PREFACE

The following pages have as their central problem the value of money. But the value of money cannot be studied successfully as an isolated problem, and in order to reach conclusions upon this topic, it has been necessary to consider virtually the whole range of economic theory; the general theory of value; the rôle of money in economic theory and the functions of money in economic life; the theory of the values of stocks and bonds, of "good will," established trade connections, trade-marks, and other "intangibles"; the theory of credit; the causes governing the volume of trade, and particularly the place of speculation in the volume of trade; the relation of "static" economic theory to "dynamic" economic theory.

"Dynamic economics" is concerned with change and readjustment in economic life. A distinctive doctrine of the present book is that the great bulk of exchanging grows out of dynamic change, and that speculation, in particular, constitutes by far the major part of all trade. From this it follows that the main work of money and credit, as instruments of exchange, is done in the process of dynamic readjustment, and, consequently, that the theory of money and credit *must be a dynamic theory*. It follows, further, that a theory like the "quantity theory of money," which rests in the notions of "static equilibrium" and "normal adjustment," abstracting from the "transitional process of readjustment," touches the real problems of money and credit not at all.

This thesis has seemed to require statistical verification, and the effort has been made to measure the elements in trade, to assign proportions for retail trade and for wholesale trade, to obtain *indicia* of the extent and variation of speculation in securities, grain, and other things on the organized exchanges, and to indicate something of the extent of less organized speculation running through the whole of business. The ratio of foreign to domestic trade has been studied, for the years, 1890-1916.

The effort has also been made to determine the magnitudes of banking transactions, and the relation of banking transactions to the volume of trade. The conclusion has been reached that the overwhelming bulk of banking transactions occur in connection with speculation. The effort has been made to interpret bank clearings, both in New York and in the country outside, with a view to determining quantitatively the major factors that give rise to them.

In general, the inductive study would show that modern business and banking centre about the stock market to a much greater degree than most students have recognized. The analysis of banking assets would go to show that the main function of modern bank credit is in the direct or indirect financing of corporate and unincorporated *industry*. "Commercial paper" is no longer the chief banking asset.

It is not concluded from this, however, that commerce in the ordinary sense is being robbed by modern tendencies of its proper banking accommodation, or that the banks are engaged in dangerous practices. On the contrary it is maintained that the ability of the banks to aid ordinary commerce is increased by the intimate connection of the banks with the stock market. The thesis is advanced—though with a recognition of the political difficulties involved—that the Federal Reserve Banks should not be forbidden to rediscount loans on stock exchange collateral, if they are to perform their best services for the country.

The quantity theory of money is examined in detail, in various formulations, and the conclusion is reached that the quantity theory is utterly invalid.

The theory of value set forth in Chapter I, and presupposed in the positive argument of the book, is that first set forth in an earlier book by the present writer, *Social Value*, published in 1911. That book grew out of earlier studies in the theory of money, in the course of which the writer reached the conclusion that the problem of money could not be solved until an adequate general theory of value should be developed. The present book thus represents investigations which run through a good many years, and to which the major part of the past six years has been given. On the basis of this general theory of value, and a dynamic theory of money and exchange, our positive conclusions regarding the value of money are reached. On the same basis, a psychological theory of credit is developed, in which the laws of credit are assimilated to the general laws of value.

In a final section, the constructive theory of the book is made the basis for a "reconciliation" of "statics" and "dynamics" in economic theory—an effort to bring together the abstract theory of price (*i. e.*, "statics") which has hitherto chiefly busied economists, and the more realistic studies of economic change (*i. e.* "dynamics") to which a smaller number of economists have given their attention. These two bodies of doctrine have hitherto had little connection, and the science of economics has suffered as a consequence.

This book was not written with the college student primarily in mind. None the less, I incline to the view that the book, with the exception of the chapter on "Marginal Utility," is suitable for use as a text with juniors and seniors in money and banking, if supplemented by some general descriptive and historical book on the subject, and that the whole book may very well be used with such students in advanced courses in economic theory. I think that bankers, brokers, and other business men who are interested in the general problems of money, trade, speculation and credit, will find the book of use. Naturally, however, it is my hope that the special student of money and banking, and the special student of economic theory will find the book of interest. The book may interest also certain students of philosophy and sociology, who are concerned with the applications of philosophy and social philosophy to concrete problems.

My obligations to others, running through a good many years, are very great. With Professor E. E. Agger, I talked over very many of the problems here discussed, in the course of two years of close association at Columbia University, and gained very much from his suggestions and criticisms. Professor E. R. A. Seligman has read portions of the manuscript, and given valuable advice. Professor H. J. Davenport has given the first draft an exceedingly careful reading, and his criticisms have been especially helpful. Professor Jesse E. Pope supervised my investigations in the quantity theory of money in 1904-5, in his seminar at the University of Missouri, and gave me invaluable guidance in the general theory of money and credit then. More recently, his intimate first hand knowledge of European and American conditions, both in agricultural credit and in general banking, has been of great service to me. Mr. N. J. Silberling, of the Department of Economics at Harvard University, has been helpful in various ways, particularly by making certain statistical investigations, to which reference will be made in the text, at my request. Various bankers, brokers, and others closely in touch with the subjects here discussed have been more than generous in supplying needed information. Among these may be especially mentioned Mr. Byron W. Holt, of New York, Mr. Osmund Phillips, Editor of the *Annalist* and Financial Editor of the *New York Times*, Messrs. L. H. Parkhurst and W. B. Donham, of the Old Colony Trust Company in Boston, various gentlemen in the offices of Charles Head & Co., and Pearmain and Brooks, in Boston, Mr. B. F. Smith, of the Cambridge Trust Company, Mr. W. H. Aborn, Coffee Broker, New York, Mr. Burton Thompson, Real Estate Broker, New York, Mr. Jas. H. Taylor, Treasurer of the New York Coffee Exchange, Mr. J. C. T. Merrill, Secretary of the Chicago Board of Trade, DeCoppet and Doremus, New York, and Mr. F. I. Kent, Vice President of the Bankers Trust Company, New York. My greatest obligations are to two colleagues at Harvard University. Professor F. W. Taussig has given the manuscript very careful consideration, from the standpoint of style as well as of doctrine, and has discussed many problems with me in detail. Professor O. M. W. Sprague has placed freely at my service his rich store of practical knowledge of virtually every phase of modern money and banking, and has read critically every page of the manuscript. None of these gentlemen, of course, is to be held responsible for my mistakes. I also make grateful acknowledgment of the aid and sympathy of my wife.

In the course of the discussion, frequent criticisms are directed against the doctrines of Professors E. W. Kemmerer and Irving Fisher, particularly the latter, as the chief representatives of the present day formulation of the quantity theory. Both their theories and their statistics are fundamentally criticised. I find myself in radical dissent on all the main theses of Professor Fisher's *Purchasing Power of Money*, and at very many points of detail. To a less degree, I find myself unable to concur with Professor Kemmerer. But I should be sorry if the reader should feel that I fail to recognize the distinguished services which both of these writers have performed for the scientific study of money and banking, or should feel that dissent precludes admiration. I acknowledge my own indebtedness to both, not alone for the gain which comes from having an opposing view clearly defined and ably presented, but also for much information and many new ideas. My general doctrinal obligations in the theory of money and credit are far too numerous to mention in a preface. My greatest debt in general economic theory is to Professor J. B. Clark.

B. M. ANDERSON, JR.

HARVARD UNIVERSITY, March 31, 1917.

PART I. THE VALUE OF MONEY AND THE GENERAL THEORY OF VALUE

THE VALUE OF MONEY

CHAPTER I

ECONOMIC VALUE

The problem of the value of money is a special case of the general problem of economic value. The present chapter is concerned with the general theory of value, while the rest of the book will consider the numerous peculiarities and complications which make money a special case. The main proof of the theory here presented is to be found in a previous book[1] by the present writer. A number of periodical articles by several writers which have since appeared, in criticism or in further development of the theory, have at various points led to shifting emphasis and clearer understanding on the author's part, and the present exposition, without seeking explicitly to meet many of these criticisms, or to embody the new developments, will none the less be different because of them. To one writer in particular, Professor C. H. Cooley, the theory is indebted for restatement, amplification, and important additions.[2] On the whole, however, the theory presented in this chapter is substantially the theory presented in the earlier book. The theory is set forth in the present chapter with sufficient fullness to make the present volume independent of the earlier book.

Value has long been recognized as the fundamental economic concept. There have been many and divergent definitions of value, and many different theories as to its origin. It is the belief of the present writer—not shared by all his critics!—that the definition of value which follows, and the conception of the function of value in economic theory involved in it, conform to the actual use of the term in the main body of economic literature. The theory of the *causes* of value here advanced is new, but the definition of value, and the conception of the relation of value to wealth, to price, to exchange, and to other economic ideas, seem to the present writer to conform to what is implied, and often expressed, in the general usage of economists.[3]

It is important to separate sharply two questions: one, the theory of the causes of value, and the other, the definition of value, or the question of the formal and logical aspects of the value concept. The two questions cannot be wholly divorced, but clarity is promoted by considering them separately. We shall take up the formal and logical aspects of the matter first.

Value is the common quality of wealth. Wealth in most of its aspects is highly heterogeneous: hay and milk, iron and corn-land, cows and calico, human services and gold watches, dollars and doughnuts, pig-pens and pearls—all these things, diverse though they be in their physical attributes, have one quality in common: Economic Value.[4] By virtue of this common or generic quality, it is possible to add wealth together to get a sum, to compare items of wealth with one another, to see which is greater, to get ratios of exchange between items of wealth, to speak of one item of wealth, say a crop of wheat, as being a percentage of another, say the land which produced it, etc. This common quality, value, is also a *quantity*. It belongs to that class of qualities which can be greater or less, can mount or descend a scale, without ceasing to be the same quality,—like heat or weight or length. Such qualities are *quantities*. There is nothing novel in the statement that a quality is also a quantity. It is implied in every day speech. We say that a man is tall, or heavy, or that the room is hot—qualitative statements; or we may say exactly how tall, or how heavy, or how hot—quantitative statements. The distinction between qualitative analysis and quantitative analysis in chemistry implies the same idea. Thus we may speak of a piece of wealth as having a definite quantity of value, or say that the value of the piece of wealth is a definite quantity. We may then work out mathematical relations among the different quantities of value, sums, ratios, percentages, etc.

Ratios of Exchange are ratios between two quantities of value, the values of the units of the two kinds of wealth exchanged.[5] A good many economists, particularly in their chapters on definition, have defined value as a ratio of exchange. This is inaccurate. The ratio of exchange presupposes *two* values, which are the terms of the ratio. The ratio is not between milk and wheat in all their attributes. It is between milk and wheat with respect to one particular attribute. Compare them on the basis of weight, or cubic contents, and you would get ratios quite different from the ratio which actually is the ratio of exchange. The ratio is between their values.

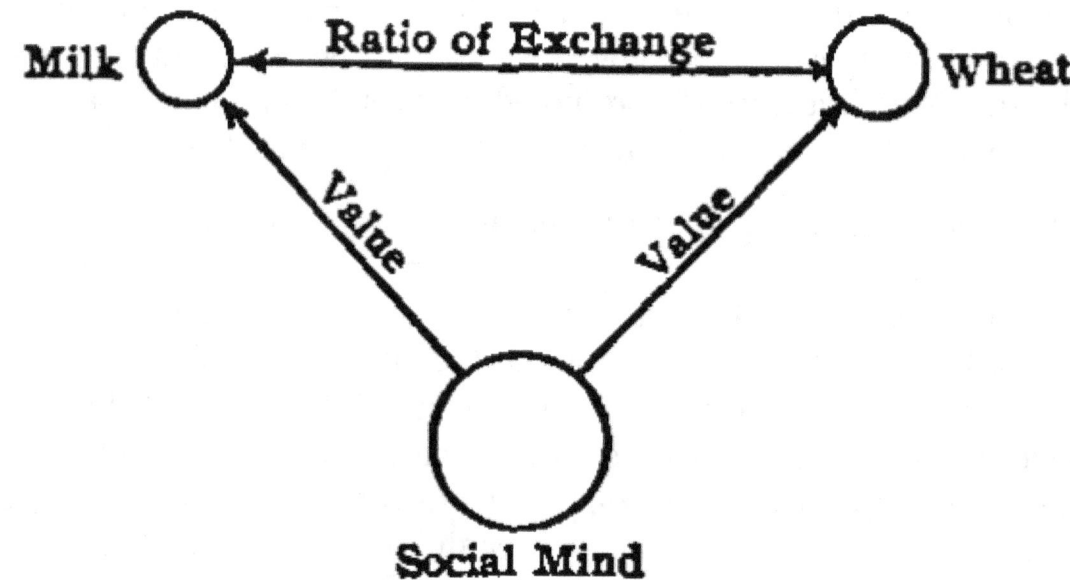

In the diagram above, something of what is to follow is anticipated, since the cause of value is indicated. Wheat is shown to be exerting an influence on milk, and milk exerts an influence on wheat. The comparative strength of these two influences determines the ratio of exchange between them. But these two influences are not ultimate. The ratio of exchange is a relation, a *reciprocal* relation. It works both ways. But behind this relativity, this scheme of relations between values, there lie two values which are absolute.

These values rest in the pull exerted on wheat and on milk by the human factor which is fundamental, which in our diagram we have called the "social mind." Values lie behind ratios of exchange, and causally determine them. The important thing for present purposes is merely to note that value is prior to exchange relations, that it is an absolute quantity, and not, as many economists have put it, purely relative. The ratio of exchange is relative, but there must be absolutes behind relations.

A *price* is merely one particular kind of ratio of exchange, namely, a ratio of exchange in which one of the terms is the value of the money unit.[6] In modern life, prices are the chief form of ratio of exchange, but it is important for some purposes to remember that they are not the only form.

Values may simultaneously rise and fall. There may be an increase or decrease in the sum total of values. Ratios of exchange cannot all rise or fall. A rise in the ratio of the value of wheat to the value of milk means a fall in the ratio of the value of milk to the value of wheat. Both may have fallen in absolute value, but both cannot simultaneously rise or fall with reference to one another. This is the truism regarding ratios of exchange which many economists have inaccurately applied to value itself in the doctrine that there cannot be a simultaneous rise or fall of values. There can be a simultaneous rise or fall of values, but not a simultaneous rise or fall of ratios of exchange.

There can be a general rise or fall of prices. Goods in general, other than money, may rise in value, while money remains constant in value. This would mean a rise in prices. Or, money may fall in value while goods in general are stationary in value. This would also mean a rise in prices. In either case, more money would be given for other goods, and the ratio between the value of the money unit and the value of other goods would have altered adversely to money. There are writers to whom the term, value of money, means merely the average of prices (or the reciprocal of the average of prices). For them, a rise in the average of prices is, *ipso facto*, a fall in the value of money. This view will receive repeated attention in later chapters. The view maintained in the present book is that the value of money is a quality of money, that quality which money shares with other forms of wealth, which lies behind, and causally explains, the exchange relations into which money enters. Every price implies *two* values, the value of the money-unit and the value of the unit of the good in question.

Value is prior to *exchange*. Value is not to be defined as "power in exchange." Certain writers[7] who see the need of a quantitative value, which can be attributed to goods as a quality, still cling to the notion that value is relative, that two goods must exist before one value can exist, and that value is "power in exchange," or "purchasing power." The power is conceived of as something more than the fact of exchange, and as a cause of the exchange relations, but is, none the less, defined in terms of exchange. This position, however, does not really advance the analysis. It is a verbal solution of difficulties merely. To say that goods command a price because they have power in exchange is like saying that opium puts men to sleep because it has a dormitive power. Physicians now recognize that this is no solution of difficulties, that it is merely a repetition of the problem in other words. If we wish to explain exchange, we must seek the explanation in something anterior to exchange. If value is to be distinguished from ratio of exchange at all, it cannot be defined as "power in exchange."

To seek to confine value to exchange relations, moreover, makes it impossible to speak of the value of such things as the Capitol at Washington City, or the value of an entailed estate, or of values as existing *between* exchanges. Nor can we make the price which a good would command at a given moment the test of its value, except in the case of the highly organized, fluid market. Land, at forced sale, notoriously often brings prices which do not correctly express its value. Moreover, even for wheat in the grain pit, the exchange test is valid only on the assumption that a comparatively small amount is to be sold. If very much is put on the market, the situation is changed, and the value falls. In other words, if "bulls" cease to be "bulls," and shift to the other side of the market, the very elements which were sustaining the value of the wheat have been weakened, and of course its value falls. "Power in exchange" is a function of two factors, (1) value and (2) saleability. A copper cent has high saleability, with little value, while land has high value with little saleability.[8] Some things have value with no saleability at all. In a socialistic community, where all lands, houses, tools, machines, etc., are owned by the state, and where such "prices" as exist are authoritatively prescribed, value and exchange would have no necessary connection. Values would remain, however, guiding the economic activity of the socialistic community, directing labor now here, now there, determining the employment of lands now in this sort of production, now in that. Exchange is only one of the manifestations of value. More fundamental, and more general, including "power in exchange," but not exhausted by it, is the power which objects of value have over the economic activities of men. This is the fundamental function of values. The entailed estate, which cannot be sold, still has power over the actions of men. The care which is taken of it, the amount of insurance which an insurance company will write on it, etc., are manifestations and measures of its value. The same may be said of the Capitol at Washington.[9]

In the fluid market, prices correctly express values. Assuming that the money-unit is fixed in value, variations in prices in the fluid market correctly indicate variations in values. The great bulk of our economic theory, the laws of supply and demand, cost of production, the capitalization theory, etc., do assume the fluid market, and a fixed value of the dollar.[10] Our economic theory is static theory, in general, and abstracts from the time factor and from "friction." In fact, values change first, and then, more or less rapidly, and more or less completely, prices respond. In the active wholesale and speculative markets, where the overwhelming bulk of exchanging takes place, the prices respond quickly. Static theory is thus adequate for the explanation of these prices, for most practical purposes, so long as the changes in prices are due to changing values of goods, rather than to changing value of the money-unit. Moreover, the distinction between value and price is, in a fluid market, where the value of money is changing slowly, often not important. In the assumption of money, and of a fixed value of money, the absolute value concept is already assumed. No harm is done, however, if the economist does not explicitly refer to this, but goes on merely talking about money-prices. Very many economic problems indeed may be solved that way. This is why the inadequate character of the conceptions of value as "ratio of exchange" or "purchasing power" has not prevented these notions from being serviceable tools in the hands of many writers. But there are many problems for which these conceptions are not adequate, because the implicit assumption of a fixed value of money cannot be made. Among these problems is the problem of the value of money itself, which constitutes the subject of this book. For that problem, an absolute value concept is vital.

If, in our diagram above, we substitute for "social mind" the more general expression, "human factor," we should find that our value concept is the common property of many writers. We should find it fitting in with the absolute value notion of Adam Smith and of Ricardo.[11] The "human factor" which *explains* the absolute value is, for them, labor. We should find it fitting in with the "socially necessary labor time" of Marx: the value of a bushel of wheat is the amount of labor time which, on the *average*, is required to produce a bushel of wheat. It is an absolute value. It is a causal coefficient with the absolute value, similarly explained, of the bushel of corn, in explaining the wheat-price of corn. Our concept will fit in exactly with the "social use-value" of Carl Knies, according to whom the economic value of a good in society is an *average* of its varying use-values to different individuals in the market. This average is an absolute quantity. The absolute values of units of two goods, thus explained, causally fix the exchange ratio between the goods. Knies' value-theory, it may be noticed, is explicitly modeled on that of Marx, to whom he refers, the difference being that Knies takes an average of individual use-values, while Marx takes an average of individual labor-times, as the causal explanation.[12] Our value concept will fit perfectly with Professor J. B. Clark's "social marginal utility" theory of value. Indeed, the present writer gratefully acknowledges that the concept is Professor Clark's rather than his own, and that all that is necessary for its explanation has been set forth by Professor Clark.[13] Professor Clark's *causal* theory of value, his explanation of this absolute quantity of value as a *sum* of individual marginal utilities, we have elsewhere[14] criticised as involving circular reasoning, like all marginal utility theories, in so far as they offer causal explanations. But his statement of the logical character of value, of the relation of value to wealth, of value to price, of value to exchange, of the functions of the value concept in economic theory, and of the functions of value in economic life,—Clark's doctrines on these points we have accepted bodily, and in so far as the present writer has added anything to them it has been by way of elaboration and defence.

The concept of value here developed is explicitly adopted by T. S. Adams, David Kinley, W. A. Scott, W. G. L. Taylor, L. S. Merriam, and A. S. Johnson, among American writers, to name no others. All of these writers would concur in the formal and logical considerations[15] as to the nature of value here presented, whatever differences might appear among them as to the causal explanation of value.

The value concept here presented performs the same logical functions as the "inner objective value" of Karl Menger, Ludwig von Mises, and Karl

Helfferich, discussed in our chapter on "Marginal Utility," below, and is, in its formal and logical aspects, to be identified with that notion. It is essentially like Wieser's "public economic value," discussed in the same chapter.[16] That there should remain critics[17] who consider the present writer a daring innovator, who is thrusting a personal idiosyncracy in terminology upon economic theory, is striking evidence that men often talk about books which they have not read! The reader who accepts, provisionally, the doctrine so far presented, as a tool of thought which will aid us in the further progress of the argument, may do so with the full assurance that he is accepting a tried and tested concept, which has seemed necessary to very many indeed of the great masters of the science.[18]

So far, the writer feels himself in accord with the main current of economic thought. When we come to a causal explanation of the value quantity, however, earlier theories appear unsatisfactory. The labor theory of value has long since broken down, and has been generally abandoned. The reasons for this will appear in the chapter on "Cost of Production." The effort to explain value by marginal utility, by the satisfactions which individuals derive from the last increment consumed of a commodity, has likewise broken down, as will appear in the chapter on "Marginal Utility." In general, it may be said that the effort to pick out feeling magnitudes,[19] either of pleasure or pain, in the minds of individuals, and combine them into a social quantity, leads to circular reasoning. Thus, the utility theory: It is not alone the intensity of a man's marginal desire for a good which determines his influence on the market. If he has no money, he may desire a thing ever so intensely without giving it value. If he is rich, a slight desire counts for a great deal. In other words, utility, backed by *value*, gives a commodity value. But this is to explain value by value, which is circular. So with the theory of average labor *time*. How shall we average labor time? The problem is easy if we confine ourselves, say, to wheat. If one bushel of wheat is produced with ten hours' labor, a second with eight hours' labor and a third with six hours' labor, the average is eight hours, and we may fix the value of the bushel of wheat according. But suppose we wish to compare the labor engaged in making *hats* with the labor engaged in raising wheat. How can such labor be compared? Hats are, in their physical aspects, incommensurable with wheat. The one quality which they have in common, relevant to the present interest, is *value*. Given the value of the wheat and the value of the hats, you may compare and average out the labor engaged in producing them. But if value must be employed as a means of averaging labor, it is clear that average labor can be no explanation of value. This is not the only flaw in the labor-time theory, but it illustrates a vice which it has in common with all those theories which start with individual elements, and seek to combine them into a social quantity. The whole method of approach is wrong. It makes two abstractions, neither of which is legitimate: first, it abstracts the individual from his vital and organic connections with his fellows, and then, second, it takes from the individual, thus abstracted, only a small part, that part immediately concerned with the consumption or production of wealth. In this process of abstraction, very much of the explanation of value is left out. The *whole* man, in his *social* relations, must be taken into account before we can get an adequate theory of value. We turn, then, to a brief discussion of society and the individual, and to a discussion of those individual activities and social relations which are most significant in the explanation of economic value.

All mental processes are in the minds of individual men. There is no social "oversoul" which transcends individual minds, and there is no social "consciousness" which stands outside of and above the consciousnesses of individuals. So much by way of emphatic concurrence with those critics of the social value theory[20] who persist in foisting upon the theory the notion that there is a social oversoul, or that the "social organism" is some so far unclassified biological specimen. To say that economic value is a social value, the product of many minds in organic interplay, is not to say that economic value is independent of processes in the minds of individual men, or that it results from any mysterious behavior of a social oversoul.

The human animal is born with certain innate instincts and capacities. Human animals of different races and different strains are in highly important points different in their instincts and capacities. But the human animal is not born with a *human mind*. Nor could the human animal, apart from association with his fellows, ever develop a human mind. "The human mind is what happens to the human animal in a social situation."[21] Of course, without the care of adults, the infant would, in general, promptly perish. But, more fundamental for our purposes, is the fact that all the important stimuli which play upon the child during his first two years, when the human mind is being developed, are social stimuli. So true is this, that the child's commerce with physical things runs in social terms. The child interprets the physical objects about him *personally*, attributes life and human attributes to them, holds conversation with them, praises and blames them, makes companions of them. This *animism* of the child, so puzzling to an old-fashioned psychology, is readily explained by social psychology. It is a social interpretation of the universe. It follows naturally from the principle of apperception: the interpretation of the unknown in terms of the known; the extension of accumulated experience to the interpretation of new experiences. The first experiences of the human animal are social experiences.

In the history of human society, a similar generalization is possible. The human *individual* is found, not in primitive life, but late in the scale of social evolution. Individuality is a social product. The savage is not a free, self-conscious person, who can set himself off against the group, and feel himself an isolated centre of power. His life is wrapped up in the group life. In the great barbarian states like Ancient Egypt or China, the life of the individual was so controlled by social tradition, and innovation was so ruthlessly crushed out that individuality had little scope. Greece and Judea gave larger scope to individual variation, but the individual still felt himself bound up with his group, and was stoned, given hemlock, or crucified if he challenged the existing social order too seriously. The break-up of the Greek city states, as independent sovereignties, and their subjection to the universal sway of Rome, made it possible for the cultured Greek to set himself up in opposition to the State; the coming of Christianity, substituting personal relations with deity, for the communal worship which had preceded it, gave the individual a vital interest apart from the life of the group about him, so that he could still further feel independent of his immediate social environment. The development by the Roman lawyers of the *Jus Gentium*, the law which is common to all nations as distinguished from the particular law of a given group, emphasized the doctrine of the Christian religion and of the Stoic philosophy of a humanity which transcends the limits of a given state,[22]—a notion which tended to free the individual from dependence on his immediate associates. But note that in all this we have merely a widening and multiplying of social relationships, and that the individual gains freedom from one set of social relationships only by coming into others. The

Christian gains freedom from his immediate surroundings because he feels himself in communion with "angels and archangels and all the glorious company of Heaven." Francis Bacon could survive his degradation in the England of his day because he could leave his "name and memory ... to foreign nations and to the next age."

Bagehot, in his *Physics and Politics*, Tarde, and Baldwin, to name no others, [23] have shown how tremendously responsive human beings are to suggestion, how wide is the sway of imitation in human life, how fashion, mode, custom, etc., make and mold the individual. Cooley,[24] with an improved psychology, has amplified the analysis, tracing the development of the individual mind in interaction with the minds of those about him, making still clearer the sweep and pervasiveness of social factors in framing the very self of the individual. In what follows, I assume the results of these investigations. They constitute the starting point from which we set out on the quest of a theory of economic value.

So much for the individual. He is a social product. But what of society? Objective, external, constraining and impelling forces, which are not physical, which are seemingly not the products of the will of other individuals with whom the individual holds converse, meet the individual on every hand. There is the Moral Law, sacred and majestic, which stands above him, demanding the sacrifice of many of his impulses and desires. There is the Law, external to him and to his fellows, in seeming, failure to obey which may ruin his life. There is Public Opinion, which presents itself to him as an opaque, impersonal force, before which he must bow, and which he feels quite powerless to change. There are Economic Values ruling in the market place, directing industry in its changing from one sort of production to another, bringing prosperity to one individual and bankruptcy to another, not with the caprice of an individual will, but with the remorseless impersonality of wind and tide. He who conforms to them, who anticipates their mutations, gains great wealth—but no business man dare set his personal values against them. There are great Institutions, Church and State and Courts and Professions and giant Corporations and Political Parties, and multitudinous other less formal or smaller institutions, which go on in continuous life, though the men who act within them pass and change. Their Life seems an independent life, and the individual who tries to change their course finds that his efforts mean little indeed, as a rule. There is a realm of Social Objectivity, a realm of organization, activity, purpose and power, not physical in character, not mechanical in nature, which is set in opposition to individual will, purpose, power, and activity. How is the individual related to this objective social world?

Three main types of theory have sought to answer this question. On the one hand, there is a type of theory, doubtless the oldest type, a type which arises easily in a period when social changes are slow, which sees in the objective social world something really separate and distinct from individual life, having a non-human origin, and deriving its power from something other than the human will. On the other hand, there is an extreme individualism, which emphasizes individual separateness, which posits as a *datum* the individuality which we have seen to be a social product, and thinks of the objective social realm as a mere mechanical, mathematical summing up of individual factors, or as a something which individuals have consciously made, by contract or agreement, or what not. Finally, there is a type of theory, to which the present writer would adhere, which finds a false antithesis in the contrast thus sharply made between society and individual, which holds that the individual is not, in his psychological activity, so much set off from the activities of his fellows as the contrast would indicate, but rather shares in the give and take of a larger mental life. This larger mental life is completely accounted for when all the individuals are completely accounted for, but it cannot be accounted for by considering the individuals *separately*. No individual is completely, or primarily, accounted for until his *relations* to the rest of the group are analyzed. Thinkers who start out with the individuals separately conceived, and then seek to combine them in some arithmetical way, abstract from those organic social relations which constitute the very heart of the phenomenon we are seeking to explain. The parts are in the whole, but the whole is not the *sum* of the parts. The relationships are not arithmetical, additive, mechanical, but are vital and organic. Men's minds *function* together, in an organic unity.[25]

The first two of these types of theory (perhaps because individuals are *physically* sharply marked off from one another, and go on in *biological* functioning in obvious separateness) have falsely accentuated the self-dependence and separateness of individual *minds*. The second type of theory, which has sought to work out the whole thing on the basis of this false conception of the individual, has largely failed to see the objective social realities, or has, with methodological rigor, denied their existence. This second type of thinking has especially characterized a good deal of economic theory, which rests on the philosophy and psychology of David Hume.[26] We will set our doctrine in clearer light if we contrast three parallel types of theory which have appeared with reference to the nature of morality, of law, and of economic value. For each of these phenomena, we have theories which represent all three of the types of social thinking to which we have referred.

In the theory of morals, we have, at one extreme, doctrines like those of Kant and Fichte, according to whom morality is a matter of obligation, independent of the human will, independent of consequences, inherent in the nature of things. Man's mind can find out what the moral law is, but man's mind has nothing to do with the making of the moral law. The same notion is involved in the ideas of "natural rights," "justice though the heavens fall," and the like. The conception is strikingly brought out in the question about which old theologians sometimes debated: is Right right because God enjoins it, or does God enjoin Right because it is Right? Whether or not Right is supreme over God, these old theologians never questioned that Right is supreme over all human wishes and desires, and in no sense an outcome of them. At the other extreme, we have the moral doctrine of the Sophists, for whom each man's *will* was right for him—a doctrine which reappears in every individualistic and anarchistic age. For this doctrine, there are no valid social standards of right and wrong. There is nothing binding on the moral agent but his own will. In between, is the moral doctrine of such thinkers as Friedrich Paulsen, or John Dewey, who represent the reigning type of moral theory to-day. For them, morality is a purely human matter. It grows out of the needs and interests of men. What is good at one time and place is not necessarily good at another time and place. There are no immutable moral principles, valid throughout the ages. None the less, morality is not a private matter, about which men may do as they please. Morality is the product of an organic society, the product of the interplay of many minds. To a given individual, the moral law is, indeed, an external constraining and impelling force. It is the will of the rest of the group. It may be his own will too, but if it is not, it overrides his personal preference, He, on the other hand, is part of the group which constrains and guides every other individual. There are, in fact, many sets of moral values: on the one hand, the social moral values *par excellence,* which the group will *enforce* in various ways; and then, for each individual, his own moral values, which may correspond qualitatively more or less with the group values, or may antagonize them. But the Moral Law is the will of the group. It is no simple composite of the moral values of individuals. It has its organic interrelations with all phases of social life. Economic changes modify it, legal changes modify it, religious values modify it, all phases of social life are expressed in it.

In legal theory, we find these three types of doctrine also. The first type is clearly indicated in the general attitude of American and English courts, especially toward the common law, though it influences their interpretation of all law. The law is something which the mind of man may find out, but may not make. If a new situation arises, the court "finds" the law—in theory the principle "discovered" by the court was in the common law at the beginning. Of course, we know that the judge invents the rule he makes, to fit a novel case, but the judge himself will not admit it. The theory of the law and the theory of morality have developed in close connection, and the notion of "natural right" is a juristic as well as a moral idea. At the other extreme, we have from certain recent students of law the doctrine that "The Law" is a myth, that there is nothing but the particular opinion of a particular judge at a particular time. Individualism cannot go so far in legal theory as to give every individual in society a chance to put his oar in, and have a separate law for himself! The social and institutional character of law is too obvious to permit that. But individualism has gone so far in legal theory as to deny all objectivity to law except in a given decision in a particular case. In between these two extreme views, appear the views of writers like Savigny, or Professor Munroe Smith, for whom the law is a changing product of social psychology, volitional[27] rather than intellectual in character, objective enough to the individual who violates it, or the judge who seeks to pervert it, but none the less not outside the minds and interests of men. In Professor Munroe Smith's phrase, law is "that part of the social order which by virtue of the social will may be supported by physical force." [28] I venture to describe this type of legal theory as the "social value" theory of the law. In the chapter on "The Reconciliation of Statics and Dynamics," *infra*, I have cited certain opinions of Mr. Justice Holmes which apply it, and even bring into it the notions of the marginal analysis.

There are, similarly, three types of economic theory. At the one extreme we have theories of "intrinsic" value, which would place economic value outside the wills of men. The mediæval discussions of "just price" often illustrate this notion. It creeps not infrequently into judicial opinions,—to which such notions are essentially congenial! The working economist of our own day has found little use for it, but in periods when economic change was slow it suggested itself not unnaturally to men, as an explanation of the seeming impersonality of market phenomena, and as a practical idea for combatting extortion and injustice. Something of the idea is involved in a sentence of Shakspere's:[29]

> "But value dwells not in particular will;
> It holds his estimate and dignity
> As well wherein 'tis precious of itself
> As in the prizer."

At the opposite extreme would be those economists, as Professor Davenport and Jevons, who find no value for a good except in the minds of individual men, so that there may be as many different values as there are different men. That something social and objective exists in the market place can hardly be denied, but when pressed for an account of it, these writers reduce it to a bare, abstract, mathematical ratio.[30] Each individual mind is shut up within its own limits, inscrutable to other minds, and there can be no psychological phenomena which include activities in many minds, for this view. In between these two extremes, is the social value theory of the present writer. Economic value is not intrinsic in goods, independent of the minds of men. But it is a fact which is in large degree independent of the mind of any given man. To a given individual in the market, the economic value of a good is a fact as external, as objective, as opaque and stubborn, as is the weight of the object, or the law against murder. There are individual values, marginal utilities, of goods which may differ in magnitude and in quality from man to man, but there is, over and above these, influenced by them in part, influencing them much more than they influence it, a social value for each commodity, a product of a complex social psychology, which includes the individual values, but includes very much more as well. Our theory puts law, moral values, and economic values in the same general class, *species* of the *genus*, social value, alike in their psychological "stuff" and character, to be explained by the same general principles, even though differentiated in their functions, and in the extent to which they depend on various factors in the social situation. They are parts of a social system of motivation and control. They are the *social forces*, which govern, in a social scheme, the actions of men.

It may be well to suggest rough *differentiæ* which mark off these values from one another. Legal values are social values which will be enforced, if need be, by the organized *physical* force of the group, through the government. Moral values are social values which the group enforces by approbation and disapprobation, by cold shoulders and ostracism or by honor and praise. Economic values are values which the group enforces under a system of free enterprise, by means of profits and losses, by riches or bankruptcy. The group may, under a communistic or socialistic system, rely in whole or in part upon the machinery of the law; in which case economic values appear not in their own form as immediately guiding production, but as "presuppositions" of some of the legal values.

The differentiation of these types of social value may also run in terms of their *functions*,[31] though it is not so easy to mark them off here, since their functions overlap. The function of economic values is to guide and control the economic activities of men, to send labor from one industry to another, to cause one sort of thing to be produced or another, to supply the motive force which *impels* industry. Legal and moral values also directly affect industry, often working to check the results which the economic values alone would lead to—as when the law forbids the production and sale of liquor, or checks child labor, etc. The law, on the other hand, does not, primarily, in its influence on industry, seek *positively* to determine its direction. The law forbids the production of liquor, but does not decree the production of bread. The law may seek to affect industry positively, by protective tariffs, for example, which aim at the building up of certain industries, but its effects are here indirect, reached through modifications in the economic values. Economic values, on the other hand, do not primarily aim at the regulation of the conduct of men outside the market place, or the shop or the farm, etc. Economic values are not primarily concerned with making men be good husbands or good neighbors, or brave soldiers. Economic values may be used, in part, for these purposes, as when a father-in-law uses his wealth as a lever to make his son-in-law behave—or, indeed, as a bait to get a son-in-law! It is hard to find a phase of social life which is not touched by all types of social values, but it is possible, roughly, to mark off those phases of social life which are subject to primary regulation by one or the other sort of social value.

The differentiation is easier when we look at the social *institutions* which have to do primarily with the one or the other sort of value. Courts and legislatures are easily marked off from stock exchanges and banking houses. There is not so clearly an institutional nucleus for moral values, since the church has lost its control over the moral situation.

When we view the matter from the standpoint of the *objects* of value, *differentiæ* also appear. The main type of object of moral value is modes of conduct; the "type object" of economic value is physical things which men eat, wear, drink, etc., even though *quantitatively* the major part of the sum total of economic values attach to other things, instrumental goods, lands, labor, and social relations, like franchise rights, good will, which in the main reflect the values of consumers' goods;[32] objects of legal value are in large degree the same as objects of moral value, namely, modes of conduct, but moral values attach to a wider group of objects, and legal values attach to certain forms of conduct which are morally indifferent.

It is not so easy to make the differentiation when we view the thing from the standpoint of the consciousness of men who are at the centre of the situation, to whose consciousness the social values are presented. We may put at the very forefront of the economic value of oranges the gustatory feelings or desires of those who consume them; at the forefront of the moral value of a heroic rescue by a fireman the thrill that runs through the onlookers. Qualitatively, these psychological states are different, as those who have experienced both will know. But it is difficult indeed to put the difference into words. When it comes to a legal value, say the legal value of a given contract right which a man seeks to enforce in court, it is not easy to find any particular emotion or state of consciousness which is peculiar or appropriate to it. The value is so highly institutionalized and impersonal, that it seems to the court and lawyers and even the litigants to be merely a question of fact to be intellectually analyzed. Its roots are deep in human emotions, but not in the emotions, primarily, of those who are handling the transaction. Perhaps the jurist has states of consciousness we know not of. There may be a distinctively legal emotion. It seems to crop out at times when one questions, in conversation with a judge or lawyer, the infallibility of the courts. But the law does not derive its power therefrom! Rather, the law derives its power from the general consent and acquiescence and support of the mass of men, who turn over to experts the details of administering it, and who support The Law in general, rather than the rule of the *corpus delicti*, with their emotional sanction.

I think that we have here a clue to a vital point for our theory. We need not expect to find the major part of the explanation of any of these social values in the conscious emotions of those who are moved by them. In the case of the orange or the heroic act, we are, indeed, close to pretty simple human feelings and desires. In general, in the case of moral values, the individual emotion and the social value are *qualitatively* comparable, since moral values rarely take on a highly institutional character. They are more free from class or institutional control than other social values. This need not be true. Thus, the plantation negro need not feel any personal shame in the moral delinquency which he none the less hides from the "white folks" whose values he must more or less conform to. But, on the whole, moral values are much more "participation values,"[33] shared by the whole group in common, than are economic values or legal values. When we pass beyond the simple case of a consumption good, and get into the realm of the more institutional economic values, we lose all guidance from the clue of satisfactions in consumption. Just what emotion, for example, is appropriate in the presence of the four and a half per cent convertible bond of the Chesapeake and Ohio Railway Co.? If it be answered that ultimately that bond represents satisfactions in consumption, since the owner of it may spend the income for consumers' goods, or since the railroad in question carries coal which goes to Italy to be used in a cruiser which will sink an Austrian warship, thereby giving consumers' satisfactions to individuals in Italy, so that the value of the bond is ultimately reducible to specific satisfactions of given individuals, we may still hold that those satisfactions do not constitute the value of the bond, as such. Moreover, the same is true of the legal values. Ultimately, very specific human emotions are affected by the rule of the *corpus delicti*, or the rule governing pleas in *estoppel*. Both in legal and in economic values we have an elaborate and complex system of social psychological character, which can by no means be reduced to elementary desires or feelings of individuals, even though when the whole story is told, no part of the system will be found outside the minds of individual men. The point has been well put by Professor C. H. Cooley: "It would be as reasonable to attempt to explain the theology of St. Thomas Aquinas, or the *Institutes* of Calvin, by the immediate working of religious instinct as to explain the market values of the present time by the immediate working of natural wants."[34] I think that any attempt to differentiate the various kinds of social value on the basis of the type of emotion in the minds of those who have most immediately to do with them, or to explain them primarily by those emotions, is foredoomed. The law does not get its power from the emotion of the judge who gives a decision, nor does the value of a rare painting rest chiefly in the intensity of desire of the few rich connoisseurs who compete for it. Back of the judge, giving *validity* to his decision, stands the will of the group; back of the rich connoisseurs stand the legal and other social values concerned with the distribution of wealth, by virtue of which they are able to make their wants felt in the market. Both judge and connoisseur are focal points, through which stream the social forces affecting the values in question. Both are important. But the emotions and ideas of neither exhaust the psychological causation involved in the values.

This is very much more apparent when we consider the values that arise in the great speculative markets, say in the wheat pit, or the stock exchange. Those who buy and sell are primarily interpreters, students, of impersonal, social forces, seeking to adjust themselves to them, to forecast them, in such a way as to derive profit from them. Their choices and decisions are also factors. Indeed, it is possible to view the matter in such a way as to make their decisions the whole story. In the same way, it is possible to make the mind of the judge the final explanation of the legal value. But the speculators themselves are under no such illusion. They know very well that if they run counter to the facts they will lose money. And the judge knows very well that the range of arbitrary choice which he can exercise without impeachment, or at least without reversal by a higher court, is very limited. Nor is even a Supreme Court of the United States free to do its arbitrary will. Just because it is so conspicuous, and because its doings are so important, it has manifested more respect for judicial tradition, and more responsiveness to the tides of public sentiment, than any other court in the Federal Judiciary.[35]

The head of a great banking house makes a decision regarding an underwriting operation. On his decision depends the question of whether or not the securities are issued. On the issue of the new securities depends, in part, the values of the existing securities of the corporation in question, and the nature of the future employment of thousands of men and great quantities of land and capital. Tremendous power is concentrated in the hands of this banker. But it is not *his* power! He cannot exercise it in an arbitrary or capricious way. He approaches his problem in much the same spirit that the judge approaches a disputed question of law. He analyzes the factors involved. He considers the condition of the money-market, the question of the probable ease or difficulty of marketing the new securities to investors, the prospects of the business of the corporation in question, the probable future demand for its products, the stability of that demand, the personnel of the management of the corporation, the attitude of the government toward it, the nature of its other outstanding securities, with special reference to the proportion of bonds to stocks, and the amount of "fixed charges" against its earnings. He may also take into account other enterprises of similar character which he has connections with, and the question of whether or not building up the corporation in question may injure other corporations to which he has responsibilities. He looks far into the future, seeking to conserve his prestige, and unwilling to assume responsibility for an issue which investors will later lose faith in. Proximately, his decision is tremendously important, and his thoughts and feelings are of immense significance, but ultimately, *they* are determined by all manner of social considerations, and *always, the degree to which they count* in determining values depends on his weight in the economic situation, which rests (1) on his *prestige, i. e.*, the massing of beliefs and hopes of many men, (2) on his *wealth*, which rests in the legal and moral values governing distribution, and (3) on his institutional relationships, which again are psychological facts, partly legal in character. He is as much a social instrument as is the judge. Both may abuse their power. Both do at times abuse their power. But the significant point is that the power both have is social power, and is in no sense proportional to the intensity of their own emotions. It arises from the emotional power in the minds of many men.

It would be easy to elaborate the points in which morals, laws, and economic values are alike, and to show in detail that the theory of economic value is merely a special case of the general theory of social value. For our present purposes, however, it is enough to have illustrated the general doctrine, and to have set up the economic values as true social forces. It may be noticed that the effort to differentiate the different kinds of value is not altogether successful. They are not in watertight compartments in social life. It is a commonplace among students of ethics that moral values grow, in greater or less degree, out of economic factors. Indeed, the "economic interpretation of history" has as its central theme the doctrine that morality, law, and ideal values in general are governed by the economic situation.

This is a one-sided view. Moral and legal values are influenced and modified by economic forces. Legal and moral values do, in part, derive their power from economic values. But on the other hand, economic values likewise derive part of their power from legal and moral values. The "social mind" is an organic whole, in which no factors exist "pure," and in which there is constant give and take. The effort to explain moral values by a single principle, as sympathy, legal values by another simple principle, as fear, and economic values by a different simple principle, as utility, is foredoomed. It has been given up by the students of law and morals, and should be abandoned by the students of economics.

Let us consider more narrowly the main factors affecting and explaining economic social values. Let us take, first, the simplest case, that of goods and services which minister directly to human wants, goods and services "of the first order." Goods of this sort would be oranges, bread, clothing, jewels. Services of this sort would be the services of the barber, the valet, the physician, the preacher, the teacher, the actor. I abstract, in discussing these values, from the complications that grow out of the friction in retail trade, and the existence of many customary prices, and prices fixed by other than economic values, in the case of teachers, or preachers. I shall concentrate attention upon such things as oranges, bread, clothing, and jewels. The *focus* of the values of these things, and an essential condition of their existence, is their utility, that is to say, their power to satisfy human wants. Utility as used in economics does not mean usefulness in any moral sense. From the standpoint of the economist, whiskey and opium are as useful as bread, if they satisfy wants equally intense. And the economist is not concerned with the general utility of things considered in their totality. Air is more useful than jewels, but a carat of air is not as useful as a one-carat diamond. Air exists in such abundance that it does not need to be economized. Scarcity with reference to the extent of the wants involved is also essential to economic value. A combination of the ideas of utility and scarcity gives us the simple notion for which the formidable name of "marginal utility" has been devised. The marginal utility of a good to a man is the power the last, or "marginal," unit of the good which the man consumes has to give him satisfaction, or, viewed from the standpoint of the man, is the intensity of his desire[36] for, or of his satisfaction in, the final unit consumed. So far, our account of the value of the orange will seem perfectly acceptable to those accustomed to traditional discussions of the problem in the text-books. The difference is that many text-books stop at this point, leaving the impression that with the definition of marginal utility the whole value problem has been solved. For the social value theory, the conception of marginal utility is barely a starting point. Indeed, it is not even a starting point. We shall have to look both in front of it and *behind it.* Recognizing that marginal utilities to individuals are essential to economic values of consumption goods, we shall have to point out other things which are also essential, and we shall have to explain the factors determining these marginal utilities themselves.

The last point may be considered first. Men's desires are socially determined. Even the simplest, most instinctive, wants of human nature are, in their concrete manifestations, the product of social culture in overwhelming degree. Consider sex and hunger. We do not enjoy our food when our neighbors pick their teeth with their forks. This would not trouble a chimpanzee, whose *instinctive* equipment in the matter of hunger is vastly more like that of a man than is the *actual* hunger impulse of a highly civilized man like that of a savage. Civilized men will often starve rather than eat human flesh. Even when moral scruples are overcome, actual physical revulsion may prevent it. Men of different times and places wish food of special sorts, served in special ways. They wish to eat in the company of their fellows, but only of those fellows who can know and obey the ritual that is appropriate to the time and place. This is true of humble folk as of those who "dress for dinner." The ritual differs for the two sorts of people. But there is a spirit, a type of conversation, a code of etiquette, which prevails at the mealtime of virtually all men, and too serious digressions therefrom will take away the appetites of all. About the mealtime and the festal board have gathered a great host of traditions, ideals, and social activities, till they have become in verity an institution, and not the least important, by any means, of social institutions. Out of the simple instinct of sex, we have evolved many of the most precious things of our civilization, and between the sex impulse of the animal and the sex impulse of the gentleman who is seeking to marry the one woman in all the world, there is a difference so great that comparison between the two is difficult.

Here we have wants which grow out of the most elementary things in human nature, wants which are intense and universal, but which vary, in their concrete manifestations, enormously from age to age and from place to place. When we come to the wants which change more quickly, the fact that social factors dominate needs no arguing. Fashion, mode, custom, obviously account for the concrete wants that exist in clothing, ornamentation, amusement, housing, etc. If we wish to know what women will be wanting to wear six months hence, we do not go to women individually and ask them. We could not find out that way. They would not know. We go rather to the theatre, and study the stage and the boxes, to the famous designers of women's dress, to the metropolitan centres of various sorts, to the "radiant points of social control"[37] from which emanate the suggestions which pass in imitative waves through the women of the country in the next few months. The laws of imitation have been elaborately developed by Bagehot, Tarde, Baldwin, Ross, LeBon, Cooley, and others, and I content myself here with referring to their writings. The wants of women—and men—are socially given, grow out of a give and take, a social process. And in this social process, it is not true that each man counts one! Rather, a few lead, and many follow. There are centres of prestige which count overwhelmingly.

Certain wants are competitive.[38] Where social status depends on having as good a house as one's neighbors, and where social leadership depends on having a better house than one's neighbors, there is no limit to men's desires for better houses. With each improvement which one introduces, each feels the desire to improve, however contented he might have been had the other not made the improvement. To this we shall recur in our discussion of the origin of money, in explaining the value of gold.

So much for the human wants which stand as the focus of economic values in the case of articles of immediate consumption.

But, given these wants, and given their marginal intensities, we are only at the beginning of our explanation of the economic values of the consumption goods. It is again not a case of each want counting one, to the extent of its intensity. There are again, by virtue of the legal and moral values governing the distribution of wealth, *centres* of power. The wants of some men count for nothing, however intense they may be. The pauper, the prisoner, the beggar—popular proverb about "beggars and horses" understands them, however much the "marginal utilitarian" may forget that their wants count for nothing.[39] The slightest whim, on the other hand, of the man who has inherited millions may count heavily in giving values to goods. For the explanation of the values of consumption goods, then, we need both the socially determined marginal utilities of individuals, and the socially determined *weight* which these individuals have in our economic system. This *weight* would involve a very elaborate explanation. Many factors affect it. We call attention here, however, especially to the fact that it rests in large part on the legal and moral values and institutions concerned with the distribution of wealth. Changes in the distribution of wealth are as important as changes in the wants themselves in giving the explanation of changes in values. The economic social values of consumption goods include not merely the values of those goods *to* the individuals who consume them, but also the values *of* the individuals themselves in the social scheme of things.

What of the values of instrumental goods, of goods of "higher orders," of labor, of stocks and bonds, of lands, of franchise rights and good will?

It is the one great contribution of the Austrian economists to have shown that the causation in value runs, primarily, from consumption goods to the goods of higher "orders" which are concerned with their production, and that these values of instrumental goods, etc., are derived and secondary values. The value of wheat is based on the value of bread, the value of land on the value of wheat. The value of the stock of United States Steel rests in part on the value of iron lands, which rests on the value of ore, which rests on the value of pig iron, which rests on the value of steel rails, which rests on the value of the service of transporting building materials, which rests on the value of a building, which rests on the value of the services which a dentist performs in an office in the building. This is the main line of causation. This is the first approximation which gives us a clue, without which we should find problems insoluble. But is it not clear that this cannot be the whole story? At every step complications enter. The whole thing cannot be got out of the value of the dentist's services, and the other consumers' goods and services, which are indirectly aided by the property to which title is given by ownership of U.S. Steel stock; nor is the value of the stock to be fully explained by the value of the property to which it gives title.

At every step, we meet the complication that men must estimate and calculate, for one thing. And rarely indeed can men see all the steps, the end from the beginning. Take first a very simple case, wheat land. The value of the wheat land of to-day rests on the value of wheat, but it is the wheat of to-morrow and for many years to come; the wheat of to-morrow rests for its value on the value of the bread of the day after to-morrow. Sometimes the differential between goods at two consecutive steps in the productive process is pretty constant. Wheat and flour vary pretty closely together. The differential is not strictly fixed even there. But bread and wheat land have a much looser connection in their variations. If land could produce no wheat or corn or other good that would satisfy human wants, and if it could not itself satisfy human wants, it would ordinarily have no value.[40] But the connection between the value of the bread and the value of the land is loose and uncertain, while the connection between the value of the land and the intensity of the wants actually satisfied by the bread produced from it, is absolutely *nil*. Whether the bread saves a starving man or feeds the pet pigeons of a millionaire, is a matter of indifference so far as the value of the land (or of the bread) is concerned.

We take the values of consumption goods, and break them up, attributing part to the labor that immediately produced them, part to the raw materials that entered into them, part to the machine that fashioned them, and so on. We then break up the value attributed to the raw material, attributing part to the labor that worked in producing it immediately, part to the machine that fashioned it, part to the rawer material of which it was made. And so with the values of the machines. Ultimately we get back to the values of labor, or of land, or of securities giving title to complexes of lands, machines, etc.— values which we do not further break up. But at every step, we find additional factors. We find these derived values becoming independent, substantial, standing in their own right. Moral and legal values affect them directly, as in the case of patriotic support of government securities, moral antagonism to the securities of the Distillers' Securities Corporation, or the influence of court decisions, legislation and elections on security values. Such values rest, in large degree, on the massing of *beliefs* and hopes, not concerned with specific satisfactions of wants, but with the existence of *future* economic values. These beliefs and hopes again have their social explanation. It is not a case where each man counts one. There are centres of prestige and power, bankers and financial magnates, whose opinions and decisions count heavily, and waves of optimism and pessimism, which affect the whole group. We shall discuss these matters more fully in connection with the analysis of credit, at a later point of our study. For the present, it is enough to point out that the whole thing cannot be explained on the basis of the values of consumers' goods, and that the values of consumers' goods are only in small part explained by the intensities of the wants they serve.

In summary: Economic value is the common quality of wealth, by virtue of which it is possible to compare divers kinds of wealth, and treat wealth quantitatively, getting ratios of exchange, sums of wealth, etc. Value is a quantity, *i. e.*, a quality which has degrees of intensity. Ratios of exchange are ratios between values. Price is a particular sort of ratio of exchange, namely, a ratio in which one of the terms is the value of the money-unit. Prices correctly express values on the assumption of the fluid market, and on the assumption that the value of the money-unit does not vary.

The value quality is psychological in character. It rests in human minds. But not in the minds of individuals thought of separately. It is a complex of many individual mental activities, highly institutionalized, and including legal and moral values, hopes and beliefs and expectations, as well as the immediate intensities of men's wants for consumption goods.

The ultimate test of scientific theory must be practice. If a theory aids in manipulating facts, if it leads to the discovery of ways of doing things which are better than old ways, if it solves problems which have hitherto remained unsolved, or carries the solution of problems farther than has hitherto been the case, it is a good theory. It need not be the best possible theory. It need not be a final theory. The chief claim for the present theory of value is that it not only unlocks all the doors that earlier theories have unlocked, but also others which have resisted the old keys. The man who goes into the modern stock market armed with marginal utility and the quantity theory is like the man who would fight Hindenburg with bows and arrows. Bows and arrows are effective in the hands of expert archers, and the great figures in the history of economics have done wonderful things with marginal utility, "real costs," and the quantity theory. But the social value theory is offered as a better weapon.

The writer believes that the problem of the value of money has not been solved by the older theories of value. He believes that the social value theory will solve it. He proposes on the basis of the social value theory to make clearer the nature of credit phenomena, and to assimilate the laws of credit to the general laws of value. He proposes with the social value theory to bring together in a higher synthesis two divergent types of economic theory, the "static" and the "dynamic." He thinks that a rigorous and consistent application of the absolute concept of value will clarify confusions at various points in the general body of price theory, as the laws of supply and demand, etc.

He offers the social value theory as the only way of giving a *psychological* explanation to the demand-curve, and a marginal *value* explanation of marginal demand-*price*. Demand-curves are social value curves, on the assumption of the fixed social value of the dollar. The utility theory, as will appear in the chapter on "Marginal Utility," has failed to give psychological magnitudes corresponding to *any* point on the demand-curve. In general, he offers the social value notion as the justification for the assumption of a quantitative value which, as we shall see, underlies the whole of our current price analysis.

The theory here outlined has been, as stated, developed and defended more fully in a previous book. For the rest, the author would have it judged by its usefulness or failure as a tool of thought in the investigations which follow.

> NOTE. It has seemed best not to break the main course of the argument of this chapter for the elaboration of one point on which there has appeared to some critics to be vagueness in the exposition of the social value theory in my earlier volume, namely, the relation of social values to the individual values of those who are moved by the social values. Social values have as their function the guidance and control of the activities of men. But men are also moved by their own individual feelings, interests, and desires.
>
> What is the relation between these two sets of factors? In what has gone before, it has been made clear that social values present themselves to

the individual as opaque, objective facts, largely beyond his control, to which he must adjust himself. They represent the minds of other men, acting in corporate and organic ways, putting pressure on him, or offering him lures. Now the individual reckons with these social values in the same way that he reckons with any other of the facts affecting the economy of his life. He must adjust himself to them in the same way that he must, if he is a blacksmith, adjust himself to the technical qualities of the iron he is manipulating. This does not mean that he is passive before them, any more than he is passive before the iron. He rather seeks to carry out his personal purposes and desires by actively adapting himself to objective facts, whatever they be. This means that different individuals will react in different ways to the same social value. The fear of the law will keep one man from burning dead leaves in the street where it will not keep another man from murder. A given degree of social pressure will make one man crease his trousers, while another man will not even know that the pressure to crease one's trousers exists! There are great individual variations in responsiveness and sensitiveness to social pressure. In part, these variations are due to inborn qualities. In larger part, they are due to social education, and to social status. Thus, the fact that one man will work all day in a ditch in response to the lure of a dollar and a half, while another will not work in the ditch for a hundred dollars a day, may rest in slight degree on the greater inborn sensitiveness of the latter to the physical pain of labor, but rests primarily on the fact that the latter doesn't need the money, and has a social standard, growing out of his class-associations and education, which would make him ashamed to be seen in the ditch. Indeed, we may think of the social standard in question as a social value acting *on* him, rather than *in* him. He fears ridicule. The same degree of social power, luring men toward the ditch, exists in the dollar in each case, but the response is very different in the two cases.

Later formulations of the utility theory and the labor cost theory, as represented by the theory of Schumpeter, which we shall discuss in the chapter on "Marginal Utility," give us, in a scheme of purely static equilibrium, a picture of the adjustment of the individual values to the social values. As we shall see, they give us no account whatever of the social values. They do not explain causation at all. But they do show that there is a tendency for the individual marginal utilities of consumption to become proportional to the social values of the goods consumed by each individual; and for the individual marginal disutilities in production to become proportional to the social values of the rewards that come to producers. The scheme is highly unrealistic. It has been emphatically repudiated by Böhm-Bawerk, so far as the disutility equilibrium is concerned. ("Ultimate Standard of Value," *Annals of the American Academy*, Vol. V, pp. 149-209.) But it is worth something, not as explaining social values or market prices, but rather, as showing how individuals *conform* to social values and market prices. *Cf. Social Value*, pp. 43-44, n. 2, and 148.

The theory that individual marginal utilities and disutilities are proportional to market values is unrealistic enough, in the light of the analysis of individual utilities which we have given, even for the utilities. It is quite impossible to make anything of importance of it from the side of individual disutilities. The length of the working day is not fixed for each worker by a comparison of his own labor pain with the satisfactions he expects from his wages. It is fixed by conditions largely external to him, and the whole group works the same number of hours, with the machine. The law may limit the working day. Trades-union effort may do it. Opportunities for alternative employment may do it, for the labor force of a factory as a whole. But the theory, which really must rest in the notion that each individual has many options, and that the working period is flexible, cannot mean much. The prosperity of the laborer does more to limit the working day than does his suffering!

The reactions of individuals as consumers or producers on the social values modify the social values. But, as we have shown, the primary explanation of the social values is not to be found in the individual utilities and disutilities of those who react to them. Utilities and labor pains are parts, but minor parts, in the explanation of social values.

CHAPTER II

SUPPLY AND DEMAND, AND THE VALUE OF MONEY

The theory of the value of money is a special case of the general theory of economic value. To the layman, this would seem to go without saying. To the student of the literature of the subject, however, who has noticed the wide divergence between the method of approach to the general problem of value and the method of approach to the problem of the value of money, in most treatises which include both these topics, the proposition will sound unusual if not heretical. Most text-books in English to-day will offer the marginal utility theory as the general theory of value. The same books commonly present the quantity theory of the value of money. Whether or not the two theories are consistent may wait for later discussion, but that the quantity theory of money is a *deduction from* the utility theory of value, and a *special case* of the utility theory of value, will not, I believe, be contended by anyone. Certainly in its origin, the quantity theory is much the older theory. The same is true for those writers who seek to explain value in general on the basis of cost of production, and who at the same time offer the quantity theory to explain the value of money. The two theories may or may not be consistent, but in any case, they are logically and historically independent, neither being a deduction from the other. Older writers (as Walker and Mill), whose treatment of the general theory of value runs in terms of "supply and demand," have stated that the quantity theory is merely a special case of the law of supply and demand, and the statement is occasionally met in present-day writings, though one of the most recent and best known of the expositions of the quantity theory, Professor Fisher's *Purchasing Power of Money*, very explicitly repudiates this doctrine.[41] But it may be easily shown, and will be shown later, that the quantity theory, and the present-day formulation of the law of supply and demand, are in no way logically dependent upon each other. This lack of connection between two bodies of doctrine which should be in a most intimate and essential way related to each other, may well throw suspicion on the current treatments of both topics. In any case the lack of connection raises a problem, and calls for explanation.

Part of the explanation may be sought in the fact that the writers who have developed the general theory of value have not been, in general, the writers who have most elaborated the theory of the value of money. The theory of money has been for a long time a more or less isolated discipline. In Ricardo, we have an elaboration of the labor theory of value, and we also have the quantity theory of money. But it is not clear that Ricardo added anything to the quantity theory. He found it, in much the form in which he used it, in the writings of predecessors, among them Locke and Hume. Ricardo makes large use of the quantity theory as a premise, but apparently feels the theory to be so self-evident that it needs little exposition or defence at his hands. John Stuart Mill is a clear exception to the general statement. Cairnes, likewise, did treat both topics in considerable detail, but while his interest in the general theory of value was that of the theorist, his treatment of money was primarily in the spirit of the publicist, and his interest was less in the justification of the theory—which he again seems to feel needs little defence—as in its application. A similar statement may be made with reference to Jevons. He worked out his general theory of value for its own sake; his utterances on the theory of the value of money must be sought scattered through his practical writings on money. Alfred Marshall's *Principles* (Vol. I) says almost nothing about the theory of money; his opinions on that subject are to be found in some *ex cathedra* replies to questions from a Parliamentary Commission. The most important discussions in England of the value of money are to be found in the long polemic between the Currency and the Banking Schools, by writers who would not be listed among the makers of the general theory of value. In the United States to-day, with the exceptions of Professors Fisher and Taussig, the writers who have been interested in the general field of economic theory have done comparatively little with the value of money (*e. g.*, Professors Clark and Fetter), and the writers who have been most interested in the value of money have usually not written largely on the general theory of value (*e. g.*, Professors Laughlin, Scott, Kinley). Professor Kemmerer might well be included as an illustration of this last statement. His primary interest is in money, rather than general theory, even though he does precede his theory of the value of money with an exposition of the utility theory of value. In German, a similar situation obtains. Böhm-Bawerk has touched the theory of money scarcely at all. Menger has written an important article on "Geld" in the *Handwörterbuch der Staatswissenschaften*, but the important thing about this article is the theory of the origin of money, and the reader will find little on the problem of the value of money. Wieser has recently taken up the value of money (in articles published in 1904 and 1909), but no trace of his views has as yet manifested itself in the English literature on money, and the writer may here express the opinion that Wieser's contributions to the theory of money are not likely to be very influential, or to add to his reputation.[42] Austrian writers on the value of money, as Wieser and von Mises, have recognized more clearly than anyone in America or England, the essential dependence of the theory of the value of money on the general theory of value. The German writer on money who has attracted most attention recently, however, G. F. Knapp, troubles himself about the general theory of value not at all.

But the main explanation of the hiatus between the two bodies of literature and doctrine is to be sought in something more fundamental. Neither utility nor costs nor supply and demand furnishes an adequate basis from which the quantity theory, or any other theory of the value of money can be deduced. The cost theory, and the supply and demand theory, in their present-day formulation, are really not theories of value at all, but are theories of *prices*, theories which presuppose *value*, and *money*, and a *fixed value of money*. And the utility theory, as usually presented, is either a theory of barter relations, or else (more commonly) speedily settles down into the grooves of supply and demand, leaping by means of a confusion of utility curves and demand-curves (or sometimes by a deliberate identification of them, *e. g.*, Flux and Taussig[43]) to the treatment of market prices. I shall take up these points in order.

A historical summary of the development of the notions of supply and demand will aid the exposition. It may be noticed, first of all, that supply and demand is really a very superficial formula even though an exceedingly useful one. By virtue of its superficial character, it antagonizes few other theories, and it has been the common property of almost all schools of value theory. Cost theories and utility theories, labor theories, or social value theories, all find use for it, in one form or another. It is really quite neutral and colorless, so far as the ultimate questions of value-causation are concerned. The more fundamental causal factors offered by one theory or another are commonly supposed to operate *through* supply or demand, in price-determination. Adam Smith seems to see this more clearly than does Ricardo. Ricardo, indeed, sometimes thought of demand and supply as forces antithetical to the forces of labor-costs which he was considering. In ch. xxx of his *Principles of Political Economy and Taxation* (ed. McCulloch, pp. 232ff.) he holds that his natural value ultimately rules, except (p. 234) in the case of monopolized articles. Supply and demand govern the prices of monopolized articles and of all articles in the short run. I do not find in Ricardo any clear statement to the effect that cost of production operates *through* influence on supply. Neither Adam Smith nor Ricardo felt the need of very much precision in the definition of supply and demand. Smith does, indeed, distinguish "effectual" from "absolute" demand, in a well-known passage (ed. Cannan, I, p. 58), defining effectual demand as the demand of the effectual demanders, *i. e.*, these who are willing to pay the "natural price" of the commodity. The term "supply" he does not use in this passage, but speaks of the "quantity which is actually brought to market," and gives as the law of market price that it is determined by the "proportion" between this quantity and the effectual demand. That much is wanting in this analysis will be sufficiently clear when the views of J. S. Mill and Cairnes are considered. Ricardo offers even less than Smith in the way of definition. The reader may compare the pages in *Ricardo's Works* cited above, and the discussion of the demand for labor on p. 241 in the same volume.

In J.S. Mill, a clean-cut notion first appears. The doctrine that price is determined by a ratio between effectual demand (*i. e.*, the wish to possess combined with the power to purchase) and supply (*i. e.*, the quantity available in the market), is sharply criticised. How have a ratio between two things not of the same denomination? "What ratio can there be between a quantity and a desire, or even a desire combined with a power?" To make supply and demand comparable, demand must be defined as "quantity demanded," and then the difficulty arises that the quantity demanded will vary with the price, which seems to present a case of circular reasoning if demand is to be a determinant of price. The solution which Mill develops for this difficulty really gives us our modern conception, virtually complete except that Mill does not present it in the useful diagrammatic form and does not whisper the magic word, "margin." There is a demand-schedule, which, plotted, would give a demand-curve. At such and such prices, such and such quantities are demanded, or will be purchased. There is a supply schedule, presenting a supply situation of similar character (though not so clearly indicated). The price reached is that price which *equalizes* amount demanded and amount supplied. A higher price will lead to competition among sellers, forcing down the price, a lower price will lead to competition among buyers, forcing up the price. The notion of a *ratio* between supply and demand is replaced by the notion of an *equation* between them. The present writer wishes to remark, in this connection, that Böhm-Bawerk's elaborate analysis, with his "marginal pairs," etc., has not advanced one step beyond this conception of Mill's, that it is really less satisfactory than Mill's analysis, because of the impedimenta of pseudo-psychology it has to carry, and because of its confusion of utility schedules with demand schedules.[44] In our present-day expositions, as presented in the diagrams, we are accustomed to say that price is fixed when marginal supply-price and marginal demand-price are equal, putting the stress on the ordinate, rather than on the abscissa, on the identity of the dollars paid or received, rather than on the identity of the goods given or received. But this is merely another way of stating the same equilibrium which Mill perceived—when marginal demand and supply prices are equal, amount supplied and amount demanded will be equal, and conversely.

One point is to be added, making explicit what is implicit in the modern theory of supply and demand. Supply and demand doctrine assumes *money*, and a *fixed value* of money. That there should be a given schedule of money-prices for varying quantities of a good, is possible only if there be a given value of the money-unit.

That the modern doctrine of supply and demand necessarily involves the assumptions of value, of money, and of a fixed value of money, may be proved by the following considerations:

Supply-situation, represented by the supply-curve, and demand-situation, represented by the demand-curve, are conceived of as antithetical and independent causal forces, whose equilibrium determines both "supply and demand" (in the sense of quantities supplied and demanded) and price. Mill's doctrine that supply and demand determine price gets out of the circle that demand (amount demanded) is itself dependent on price, only by making both demand in this sense and price *results*, rather than causes, and by putting the causation back into the more complex factors which I call "supply-situation" and "demand-situation." The two independent causes, then, are summed up in the supply-curve and the demand-curve. But, first, these curves are expressed in money. And second, a change in the value of money would affect *both* of them proportionately. But a theory which is concerned with supply and demand as independent and antithetical must abstract from factors which give them a *common* movement, without modifying their *relation* to each other. A change in the value of money would lead the supply-curve to move to the right, and the demand-curve to move to the left, the change in each being proportionate, and the amount supplied, and amount demanded, would remain unchanged. Changes in the value of money must, therefore, be abstracted from.

Again, we must precise the notion of an *increase* in demand, or of supply. Increase in demand may mean mere increase in amount demanded, consequent upon a lower price, consequent, *i. e.*, upon a lowering of the supply schedule. In this sense, increase in demand is a passive fact, a result rather than a cause. On the other hand, if the increase in demand is an increase in the amount demanded at the *same* price, if it means a change in the demand-situation, represented by the moving to the right of the demand-curve, we have a causal factor in increase in demand, a factor which raises the price and compels new supply to come into the market. We may distinguish these two meanings as increase in demand in the active and in the passive senses. *Mutatis mutandis*, we may speak of increase of supply in the active and passive senses. These distinctions have been made before, but it has not been clearly seen that these distinctions, and the connected doctrines, involve the assumption of a fixed value of money. But consider: it is the current doctrine that increase in demand in the active sense, the demanding of a greater amount at the same price, the moving of the demand-curve to the right, not only raises the price, but also tends to *increase the supply*. But this is true only if the *cause* of the increase in demand is not a cause which simultaneously works on supply, neutralizing that tendency. If the increase in amount demanded at a given price be due to a lowered value of money, then the same lowered value of money will reduce the supply available at that price *pro tanto*, and the new equilibrium, *cæteris paribus*, will be at a higher price, to be sure, but with the same amount supplied and demanded. "Demand" is a term which carries the connotation of motivating power in economic theory. Through demand run the forces which regulate production and supply. The function of increased demand is to induce increased supply. But the value concept, and the assumption of a fixed value of money, are needed to preserve this part of the doctrine. Without them we have no way of distinguishing a *real* increase in demand in the active sense, which does modify the adjustments in production, and alter the proportions of different supplies, from a *nominal* increase in demand in the active sense, which merely raises a money-price, without affecting supply.[45]

Another approach will lead to the same conclusion. Demand and supply-curves are not to be understood merely in terms of brute, physical quantities. They are rather curves expressing economic *significances*, manifesting *psychological* forces which lie behind them. No considerations of mere physical quantity will explain why one demand-curve should be "elastic" and another inelastic,—each curve has its own peculiarities, which are not mechanical in their nature. Demand-curves express the diminishing economic significance of goods as their quantity is increased. How economic significance is to be interpreted need not be argued here. I have elsewhere undertaken to show that the utility theory of value does not explain the economic significance which demand-curves express—that demand-curves are not utility curves. My own theory is that demand-curves are to be explained only in terms of a social psychology, that demand-curves are social-value curves. But my argument at this point does not rest on the particular type of causal theory of value one chooses. It is enough that the demand-curve be recognized as expressing economic significance, and diminishing economic significance.[46] But for the demand-curve to express variation in economic significance of a good, there is need for a unit in which to express that variation. That unit is the economic significance of the dollar, itself assumed to be invariable—as all measures must be assumed to be invariable if measurement is to mean anything. If the unit chosen vary in the course of a given investigation, the curve tells you nothing at all.

Another way of reaching the same conclusion is to say that an increase in demand in the active sense will lead to an increase in supply only if there be no corresponding increase in demand for the alternative employments of the sources of that supply, that, *e. g.*, an increased demand for wheat will lead to increased production of wheat only if there be not a corresponding increase in the demands for corn and other crops which can be raised on land and with labor and capital that would otherwise produce wheat. This is only another phase of the argument that went before, that an increase in demand due to a falling value of money would lead to a corresponding shift in the supply-curve. It is not quite the same argument, however, because that was an argument concerned with short run tendencies, resting on the assumption that the holders of supply would immediately react to a change in the value of money, whereas the argument just presented rests on the longer adjustments, based on the law of costs, as worked out by the Austrians. This point will be made clearer in the next chapter.

Yet another, and perhaps simpler, approach to the same conclusion is by pointing out that an individual, deciding to buy, must take account of the prices of other things in his budget—that individual demand-schedules would be different if market prices of other things—which depend on the value of money—were different.

The doctrine that supply and demand (and cost of production, the capitalization theory, and other elements in the current price-analysis) presuppose a fixed value of money, must be sharply distinguished from the doctrine of Professor Fisher (*Purchasing Power of Money*, ch. 8), and others, that a fixed *general price level* is assumed by supply and demand, etc. I should deny that a fixed general price level is assumed. The point rests in the distinction between value as *absolute* and value as *relative*. For my theory, it is perfectly possible for the general price level to rise, with the value of money constant, because of a rise in the values of *goods*. In a later chapter, on "The Passiveness of Prices," I shall examine the doctrine of Professor Fisher more closely, and set these two views in clearer contrast. For the present, it is enough to point out one vital difference between a rise in prices due to a fall in the value of money and a rise in prices due to a rise in the values of goods, with the absolute value of money unchanged: in the latter case, there is an increase in the psychological stimulus to industry, an increase in economic power in motivation, which energizes and increases production. In the latter case, especially when the fall in the value of money is rapid, and the rise in prices is clearly due to that cause (as in the case of Confederate paper, or the French *Assignats*), we find a reverse effect on industry. Intermediate cases, where money is falling in value, but where goods are also rising, give us intermediate results.

In what follows, I shall from time to time refer to this distinction. In my own exposition, I shall always use "value of money" in the absolute sense, as distinguished from the mere "reciprocal of the price level,"—a practice which I have sought to justify in the chapter on "Value," and in other places there referred to.[47]

The modern theory of supply and demand, then, assumes money, and a fixed value of money. It is, therefore, obviously unfitted as an instrument to solve the problem of the value of money. If supply and demand concepts are to be applied to this problem, they must be of a different sort. This was pointed out by Cairnes[48] who criticised Mill's formulation, and pointed out that Mill departed from it in three capital doctrines: in the theory of the value of money, in the theory of wages, and in the theory of international values. By the demand for money, Mill means, not the amount of *money* demanded, but the quantity of goods offered against money—a very different conception. (Mill, *Principles*, Bk. III, ch. viii, par. 2.) In what sense a quantity of goods can equal a quantity of money, or in what sense there can be a ratio between goods and money, (to recur to Mill's former problem as to the ratio between things not of the same denomination) Mill does not make clear, nor is it defensible to speak of either a ratio or an equation on the basis of Mill's system, since Mill had no absolute value concept. Cairnes seeks to reconstruct the notion of supply and demand, in such fashion as to make it possible to apply it universally, and takes up the question of the comparability of supply conceived as a quantity of goods, and demand, conceived, not as a quantity of goods, but as desire combined with the ability to pay. He concludes that in both supply and demand there is a physical, as well as a mental, element. Demand he defines as the desire for a commodity backed by general purchasing power; supply as the desire for general purchasing power, backed by the offer of a commodity. Thus he thinks he has made the two of the same denomination, so that comparison may be instituted between them, and the ideas of equation, ratio, and proportion made legitimate. By "general purchasing power," Cairnes seems to mean money and the representatives of money. It is not an abstract power, since it is the "physical" element in demand, comparable with, and of the same denomination with, the physical element in supply, a commodity. Cairnes' solution of Mill's difficulty seems to me to be merely verbal, however. First, in what way is the desire for general purchasing power in the mind of one man comparable with the desire for a commodity in the mind of another man? I pass over the supposed difficulty that knowledge of other men's emotions is impossible,[49] and emphasize simply the point that price offer, either by demander or supplier, is no test of the intensity of desire where there are inequalities in the distribution of wealth. But second: in what sense is general purchasing power, money and money-funds, of the same denomination as a commodity? Cairnes emphasizes the physical character of both. But surely they are not comparable on the basis of any physical attributes—weight, bulk, etc. Certainly if we look at the concept of demand here given, the physical aspect is simply irrelevant— gold money goes by weight, but what of paper money and credit instruments? And in what sense is even gold money physically of the same denomination with, say, wheat, or hay or base-ball tickets? Not physical quantities, but economic quantities, are relevant here; not weight or bulk, but *value*. By means of a concept of value, as the homogeneous quality of wealth, present in each piece of wealth in definite, quantitative degree, could Cairnes bring about comparability between the "physical" elements in supply and demand. But not otherwise. Only significances, values, are relevant here. Supply and demand presuppose value.

It will be interesting to consider the effort to solve the problem of the value of money by means of supply and demand on the lines employed by Mill, where demand for money is defined as quantity of goods to be exchanged, and supply of money as quantity of money times rapidity of circulation, and where physical quantities are treated as the relevant factor, no value concept of the sort here contended for being presupposed. This is, essentially, Mill's method. There is, in this conception, first the difficulty that "quantity of goods to be exchanged" is not a true quantity at all, but is a mere collection of things of different denominations, dozens of eggs, pounds of butter, gallons of milk, etc., incapable of being funded into a quantity.[50] There is, second, the difficulty that increasing the amount of any one of the items in this heterogeneous composite need not increase the "demand" for money, in the sense that it increases the "pull" on money, or tends to increase the supply of money. Yet, under the general doctrine of supply and demand, an increase in demand should be a stimulus to increase in supply. Indeed, it is easy to construct a case where an increase in the quantity of one of the items in this composite, the others remaining unchanged, would actually tend to *repel* money, to reduce the *supply* of money. Suppose that one item in America's stock of goods, say cotton, is much increased in quantity, and suppose that cotton has a highly inelastic demand-curve, so that the increased quantity sells for less money than the original quantity.[51] Suppose, too, that cotton is our chief article of export, and that the bulk of our cotton is exported. Would not the "balance of trade" tend to turn against us, so that gold would tend to leave the country, and the supply of money be reduced? There is nothing in the situation assumed to raise the prices of other goods,[52] so that they could exert a counteracting "pull" on money. Europeans, to be sure, having less to pay for cotton, could demand more of other things, and Americans paying less for cotton could demand more of other things. But, on the other hand, American producers of cotton, receiving less for their cotton—receiving precisely as much less as the others had more—could then demand less of other things, exactly as much less as the others are able to demand more. The original tendency for gold to leave the country, and the tendency for gold to leave the money-form and be used in the arts, would remain unneutralized. An "increase of demand for money," in Mill's sense, would in this case present the remarkable phenomenon of driving money away. Physical quantities are irrelevant. Psychological significances are what count.

It is interesting to note, in this connection, that some striking contradictions in quantity theory reasoning on any formulation, whether connected with the notions of supply and demand or not, are involved in this hypothesis. The illustration above gives a case where a lowered price level leads money to flow away from your country. But, on the quantity theory explanation of foreign exchange, it is *rising* price levels which drive gold away, and *falling* price levels which attract gold![53]

Mill's effort to apply the notion of demand and supply to the value of money is, then, (1) not an application of his formal doctrine of supply and demand, and (2), is a failure, leads to results contradictory to the general law of supply and demand, as soon as we take account of the peculiarities of individual commodities, and cease to look at commodities in one huge lump. Psychological forces, rather than physical quantities, are what count. Whether or not the supply and demand notion of Cairnes, reinterpreted by putting a quantitative value concept into it, could serve as a means of approach to the value of money, I shall not here argue. No one so far as I know has attempted to do the thing that way, and my own theory is best developed by another method. It is interesting to note, however, another somewhat different effort to apply the supply and demand formula. General Walker does so, including among the factors determining the demand for money, not only the quantity of goods to be exchanged, but also the *prices*[54] prevailing. Since by value of money Walker means merely the reciprocal of the price-level, this is the clearest possible case of a vicious circle. It would be a circle even if he were trying to explain the absolute value of money, as distinguished from the reciprocal of the price-level, since the former is one of the determinants of the latter. Value of money and values of goods determine prices; prices and quantity of goods determine demand for money; demand and supply of money determine value of money,—a hopeless circle.

I know no sense in which the terms, demand and supply of money, can have relevance to the problem of the value of money. There is one sense in which the terms can be used which fits in with the modern supply and demand-curves, and that is the sense in which they are used in the money market. Demand for money comes from borrowers; supply of money from lenders. The price paid is a money-price, the curves express the short time money-rates, the rental of money, in terms of money, for stated periods of time. There is a relation, later to be investigated, between the rental of money, the money-rate, and the value of money, but the two are in no sense the same. It should be noted, too, that we are here concerned with "money-funds" rather than with money in the strict sense,—distinctions and relations in this connection properly belong at another stage of our inquiry. Whenever the terms, demand and supply of money, appear in the following pages, they will be used in the sense developed in this paragraph.

Demand and supply are superficial formulæ. They cannot touch a problem so fundamental as that of the value of money.

CHAPTER III

COST OF PRODUCTION AND THE VALUE OF MONEY

When the cost theory was a labor theory, as with Ricardo, the expression, cost of production of money, could have a definite meaning. It meant the labor-cost of producing the money metal. Even in this form, it is recognized that cost of production has a looser connection with value in the case of money than in the case of most commodities, because the supply of money metal is large and durable, and the annual production affects it slowly. But cost of production theories, in the form of labor theories, or labor-abstinence-risk theories, have little standing in modern economic theory. Ricardo himself saw the break-down of the pure labor theory; and Cairnes, Ultimus Romanorum, so limited and modified the "real costs" doctrine as to leave little validity in it, even on his own showing. The prevalent doctrine of cost of production runs in terms of "money-costs"—and hence is of no use when the problem of the value of money itself is to be solved.

A brief historical sketch of the cost theory will be helpful. Costs are sometimes conceived as a cause of value, and sometimes as a measure of value. Often these two aspects are mixed, and writers shift from one notion to the other. This is particularly true of the labor theory. In Adam Smith the contention sometimes is that labor is unvarying in value, hence an admirable measure of values, and an excellent standard of long-time deferred payments. Smith compares wheat and silver from the standpoint of the constancy of their relation to labor, and concludes that wheat is the better standard in the long run, because it remains more nearly fixed with reference to labor than does silver. Sometimes Smith thinks of labor as a cause of value, and thinks of the labor that enters into the production of a good as the significant thing. At other times, the labor that goods will command or purchase is the significant thing—and here one is not clear whether he thinks of labor as a cause or as a measure. Whether labor is to be funded as labor-pain, or as labor-time, Smith does not state. Sometimes labor seems to be considered as homogeneous in its efficiency. At other times, he makes comparison between different kinds of labor as to their efficiency, and compares the efficiency of labor in different occupations. One can find nearly anything one pleases in Adam Smith on these points. At times he speaks of "labor and expense," rather than labor alone, as governing prices.

Labor-cost to the laborer would take the form of labor-pain or labor-time. To the employer, it would take the form of outlay in wages. Adam Smith never makes any definite statement of point of view here, and shifts back and forth from one to the other. He recognizes variations in labor-pain, in danger, etc., in different kinds of labor when discussing wages.

Ricardo elaborated the labor theory of value, and tried to think it through. He was too keen a logician to shift view-points with Smith's facility, and he tried to make a completed system.[55] There is some shifting from the theory of labor as a cause of value to labor as a measure of value, as in the following passage: "If the state charges a seigniorage for coinage, the coined piece of money will generally exceed the value of the uncoined piece of metal by the whole seigniorage charged, because it will require a greater quantity of labour, or, which is the same thing, the value of the produce of a greater quantity of labour, to procure it." (*Works*, McCulloch ed., 213.) In general, however, Ricardo developed a causal theory of value, quantity of labor being the basis of the absolute values of goods, their *relative* values depending on the relative amounts of labor involved in the production of each. I shall not go into the matter fully, but shall call attention to the rock on which the system split, as Ricardo himself admits. A greater or less proportion of capital works with labor in producing different things, and the value of product, in that case, varies not merely with the labor, but also with the amount of capital, and the length of time the capital is employed. How say, then, that labor alone governs value? How reduce labor-cost and capital-cost to homogeneous terms? James Mill tried to do it for him by making capital merely stored up or petrified labor, which gives up its value again in production. But this doesn't meet the difficulty, because there is a *surplus* value, over and above that explained by all the labor, including the labor which produced the machine, and the labor which produced the raw materials which entered into the machine, etc. The case of wine is a particularly obstinate case. Wine increases in value merely with the passage of time, at a rate which corresponds to the profit on capital. Ricardo finally, in correspondence with McCulloch, definitely abandons the case, stating that there are many exceptions to the proportionality between exchange value and labor-cost. "I sometimes think that if I were to write the chapter on value again which is in my book, I should acknowledge that the relative value of commodities was regulated by two causes instead of one, namely, by the relative quantity of labor necessary to produce the commodities in question, and by the rate of profit for the time that the capital remained dormant." (Davenport, *Value and Distribution*, p. 41.) But this is a "dualistic" rather than a "monistic" explanation—one element is a money-expense, or at all events a pecuniary item, while the other is a "real cost" item. The two are incommensurate and incommensurable.

Senior seeks to supply the unifying principle. "Abstinence" and labor have pain as a common element, and so are commensurable. Costs, reduced to labor and abstinence, become homogeneous again. Monism is restored. Cairnes completes the doctrine by adding risk to the real cost elements: a triune cost concept, sacrifice being the generic fact in the three manifestations.

With John Stuart Mill, in general, we have an entrepreneur view-point. Money-expenses of production, entrepreneur outlay, plus wages of management, or including wages of management, are the factors with which Mill reckons. He is no longer concerned with psychological ultimates, or real costs. Cairnes criticised Mill sharply for this. No distinction is more fundamental he holds, than that between costs or sacrifice on the one hand, and rewards on the other. Labor, abstinence and risk are sacrifices; wages, interest, profits are rewards. None the less, in cost doctrine, as in supply and demand doctrine, it is Mill's view which has prevailed. Cost as conceived by Mill is a superficial, pecuniary notion. It tells little as to ultimate causation. But it is virtually only as a pecuniary doctrine, costs from the entrepreneur view-point, that the cost doctrine is met in modern theory.

Why is this? Well, first, the real-cost doctrine simply does not square with the facts. The hardest labor does not produce the most valuable goods. Value in fact does not vary either with labor-pain or labor-time. In fact, whatever the explanation, it would seem to be truer that the relation is an inverse relation. Nor does the abstinence that pinches hardest produce the largest amount of capital. And while there is some correlation between risks and profits, the correlation is at best low and is not a correlation between psychological sacrifice and profits. Even "marginal abstinence" for a Rothschild or a Rockefeller causes no pain. It is absurd to seek to find a common element in the "abstinence" of a rich man and the pain of a poor and aged laborer. I pass over the supposed difficulty that abstinence is, in general, suffered by one set of minds, and labor-pain by a different set of minds, and hence, since men cannot compare their own emotions with the emotions of other men, there is no comparability. This subjectivistic psychology would, of course, make it equally impossible to fund labor-pains of different laborers, or to get any common denominator at all.[56] It is enough to point out that differences between rich and poor, between successful and unsuccessful, between efficient and inefficient, (apart from acquired differences which may be smoothed out by the "stored up labor-of-training" principle) make labor-pain, and marginal labor-pain, vary greatly from value, and make labor-pain, abstinence and risk quite incommensurable, and quite without fixed relation to value. Cairnes saw this in part, and developed his doctrine of non-competing groups to deal with it. Labor-pain and value vary together only when we are comparing goods produced by laborers within a competing group. Laborers in one group do not compete with laborers in another group. There is perfect competition in the capital market, however, and so capital costs ("abstinence") are perfectly correlated with value, to the extent that capital enters. Cairnes seems to think that the whole difficulty with his real cost doctrine comes from the failure of competition. In fact, however, it comes also from the inequalities in wealth. And even in his highly competitive capital market it is equally true that abstinence, or even marginal abstinence (a term which Cairnes does not use) has no constant relation to amount of capital accumulated, value produced, or interest received. The cost theory breaks down at every point when it runs in labor-abstinence-risk terms. So generally has this been recognized, that the cost theory has generally given way to the utility theory, and cost doctrine when it appears in modern economics is either the very superficial money-outlay notion of Mill, or else the Austrian cost doctrine, later to be discussed, which is still a pecuniary concept. I have elsewhere undertaken to show (*Social Value*, chs. 3-7, and the ch. on "Marginal Utility," *infra*) that these defects of the "real-cost" theory, are just as much in evidence in the utility theory. The failure of the real cost theory of value is by no means a vindication of the utility theory. Both have the same vice—the effort to combine into a homogeneous sum a lot of individual psychological magnitudes measured in money, when the money-measure has a different psychological significance for each individual, and so comparison and addition are impossible. But in any case, the real cost doctrine of the Classical School has failed, and so cannot serve as the basis of the theory of the value of money.

Obviously the money-outlay cost theory of Mill cannot explain the value of money itself. The marginal cost of producing twenty-three and twenty-two hundredths grains of gold will always be a dollar, however the dollar may vary in value. Indeed, in general, the assumption of a constant value of the money-unit is implied in the monetary cost concept. Cost curves are *supply*-curves and the reasoning already given as to the need for assuming constant value for money in the supply and demand concept will apply here. Costs function in value-determination only by checking supply. Rising costs tend to mean a lessened supply. But if the cost-curve is rising *because* of a fall in the value of money, then the demand-curve will be rising also, and production will not be checked. The general law as to the relation of cost to demand and supply assumes a fixed value of the unit of cost, the dollar.

To the Austrian economists we owe a rational theory of costs which gives the money-outlay concept more than a merely empirical basis. First, they see in costs not causes, but results. Value causation comes ultimately, not from the side of supply, but from the side of demand. I shall not now undertake a criticism of their explanation of demand. I have elsewhere criticised their confusion of demand-curves and utility-curves, and pointed out that marginal utility gives no explanation of demand. I shall recur to the utility theory of value at a later point. For the present, it is enough to point out that the Austrian theory of costs is independent of their utility vagaries, and rests best on the notion of supply and demand, as expressed in the modern curves, with the assumption of a fixed value of the money-unit. Costs consists of entrepreneur money outlay of various kinds, chiefly wages, interest, and rent. Rent is, for the Austrians, as much a cost as any other item of entrepreneur outlay. But these items of cost are not ultimate data. They are rather reflections of the positive values of the products.

Value runs from finished product to agents of production, labor, and instrumental goods, and land. Avoiding needless complications from a discussion of interest as a factor in cost—a doctrine on which the Austrians, say Wieser and Böhm-Bawerk, are not agreed,—it is enough to point out that high wages or high rents, which limit production in any given industry or establishment, are high *because* the land and labor in question have *alternative* uses, because other industries, or other competitors in the same industry, bid for them. Cost-curves, then, are reflections of demand-curves. The cost-curve of wheat, *e. g.*, is what it is because of the demand-curve for corn, for cattle, and for every other commodity that could be produced with the same labor and land. Cost doctrine thus becomes part of the general doctrine of supply and demand, and runs in pecuniary terms, assuming money, and a fixed value of money, and hence is incapable of serving as a theory of the value of money itself.

That some vaguer form of cost doctrine, where the unit of cost is, not money, but some composite commodity of things used in the production of the standard money metal, or a unit of abstract value, might be worked out, is doubtless true. Gold production, like other industry, is part of the general economic scheme, and there is some sort of equilibrium reached which draws labor and capital now away from, and now back to, the gold mine. To bring this equilibrium into the general scheme of the modern theory of costs, however, in terms precise enough to make a satisfactory theory of the value of money, is a thing which has not so far been done, and I do not have high hopes of its early accomplishment. In any case, such a theory must rest upon a positive theory of value. Cost doctrine is negative, and can never be fundamental.[57]

CHAPTER IV

THE CAPITALIZATION THEORY AND THE VALUE OF MONEY

Money is capital. A dollar is a capital-good. Money is, moreover, a durable form of capital, which gives forth its services bit by bit, and indeed, in a community where the state bears the burden of wear and tear, never ceases to give forth those services. In any case, from the standpoint of a given individual, so long as there is a limit of tolerance prescribed for legal tender, it is a matter of accident if he ever incurs a loss from the wastage of the capital instrument, money, through wear and tear. Moreover, the fact that money is "fungible," and that its use is to be found in a process which commonly returns to the owner, not the same coin, but a different coin, we may, in general, abstract from the wear and tear of the dollar, and look upon the dollar as a capital instrument which promises its owner, if he chooses to use it as capital, a perpetual annuity. The nature of this money service will be more fully described later. For the present it is sufficient to say that exchange is a productive process, that exchange creates values, in as true a sense as manufacturing does, and that money facilitates exchange in as true a sense as coal facilitates manufacturing. There is, at any given time, a demand-curve for this money service, manifesting itself in the money market, a demand for the short time use of money as a tool of exchange, and the "prices" which come out of the interaction of demand and supply in the money market are the short time "money rates" including the "call rates." These are properly to be conceived, not as pure interest on abstract capital, but as rents[58] which are to be attributed to money as a concrete tool.

Now, in general, when such rents appear, they may be capitalized. And the price of the instrument of production that bears these rents, will be the sum of the rents, discounted at the prevailing rate of interest, with considerations of risk, etc., allowed for. The reasoning of the capitalization theory is really quite simple. Take, for example, a piece of urban site land, which is expected to bring a perpetual annuity of one hundred dollars. The whole economic significance of the land is contained in its services, present and prospective. The possession of land under certain circumstances brings other services, as social prestige, than the services which can be alienated to a lessee. But in this case I am abstracting from considerations of that sort, and also from the factor of risk. The whole value of the piece of land under consideration comes from the value of the one hundred dollars a year. But these annual incomes are not all equally valuable, even though all expressed as one hundred dollars. The first one hundred dollars is due one year hence, the tenth ten years hence, the thousandth, a thousand years hence. The principle of perspective comes in—I abstain from any detailed discussion of the theory of interest, simply stating that in a general way I agree with the contention that *time* constitutes the essence of the phenomenon, or rather, the tendency to discount the future. The capital price of the land is the sum of an infinite convergent series of the "present worths" of the incomes. The formula is as follows: capital price of land = $\$100/1.05 + \$100/(1.05)^2 + \$100/(1.05)^3 \ldots + \$100/(1.05)^n$ when the rate of interest is 5%. The limit of this series, assuming the series to be infinite, is $2000, and a simple formula for calculating it under the assumptions, is to divide $100, the annual income, by .05, the rate of interest. Given the annual income, given the prevailing rate of interest, the capital price is determined. The relation may be illustrated, roughly, by the figure of a candle, a disk, and the shadow of the disk on the wall. The disk represents the annual income, the shadow on the wall the capital value, and the distance between the flame and the disk the rate of interest. Increase the distance between the flame and the disk, the rate of interest, and the shadow becomes smaller; shorten the distance, and the shadow is increased. Similarly, enlarge the disk, and the shadow is enlarged. The capital value varies directly with the annual income, and inversely with the rate of discount. Now my purpose here does not involve a detailed examination of the validity or limitations of the capitalization theory. For the present, the only question is, has this theory any application at all to the problem of the value of money? It offers itself as a general theory of the values of durable bearers of income. Money is a durable bearer of income.

The capitalization theory, however, is of no use for the purpose in hand. Money does not obey the general law in the relation which the magnitude of the income bears to the rate of interest. In general, the income and the rate of discount are independent variables. Their influence, operating in opposite directions, fixes the capital value, increasing income increasing the capital value, increasing discount rate reducing it. In the case of money, however, the two factors are not independent. The short time money rate is not, to be sure, identical with the long time rate of interest, which is the rate of discount for the purpose in hand. But the two tend to vary together in the long run average in fact, and they are related in the *expectation* of those who are concerned in the capitalization process.

In our chapter on the "Functions of Money," in Part III, it will be shown that normally there tends to be a difference between the money rates and the long time interest rates, the long time rates tending to be higher than the rates on short loans, the rate on very short loans being lower than the rate on somewhat longer short time loans, and the call loan rate being lowest of all. The explanation of this must be deferred till we have analyzed the functions of money. But the important thing, for present purposes, is that the money rates, though lower than the "pure rate" of interest, tend to vary, in long time averages, with that "pure rate,"[59] and that, consequently, the income from renting money, and the discount rate to be applied in capitalizing that income, are not independent magnitudes, but tend to vary together. They thus tend to neutralize one another. If money rates go up, and if they are expected to stay up long enough to justify (on the ordinary capitalization theory) a rise in the capital value of money, we have a counteracting influence in the long time interest rate, which also rises, and tends to pull down the capital value of money. To recur to our illustration of the candle and the disk, as the disk increases in diameter, the distance between the candle and the disk grows greater, and so the *shadow* tends to remain the same.

There is a further difficulty, to which attention will be called more fully in later chapters, particularly the chapter on "Dodo Bones," and the chapter on the "Functions of Money." In other cases, in general, the capital value is, as the capitalization theory requires it to be, a true shadow, a passive function of the income and the discount, of the disk and the distance between the candle and the disk. In the case of money, however, the income is causally dependent, in part, upon the capital value. Money can function as money only by virtue of having value. The shadow becomes substance in the case of money. It is the *value of money* which makes possible the *money work*. The capitalization theory, thus, if applicable at all, must be radically modified before being applied. We shall subsequently, in the chapters above referred to, take account of this fundamental complication. For the present, we can state it merely as a problem: how can we construe the interaction of the income value of money and the capital value of money in such a way as to avoid a circular theory?

But further, the capitalization theory, as heretofore formulated, like the doctrines of supply and demand and cost of production, assumes *money*, and a *fixed absolute value* of money. This assumption must be made if we are to be able to predict, on the basis of the capitalization theory, that a given annual income, at a given rate of discount, will give a specified capital value. This may be shown by the following considerations: If men anticipate that the value of the income, which is a fixed sum of dollars, is to grow less in the future, then the present worth of the bearer of that income will shrink to an extent greater than the "pure rate" of interest would call for. The principle of "appreciation and interest" comes in. The nominal interest, in times of falling value of money, tends to exceed the pure rate by an amount which compensates for the loss in value of future income as the dollar falls in value. We have here, however, a principle different from the principle of time discount. It is not the influence of time, which makes a *given* value appear smaller as it is further removed in time, but it is an anticipated lessening in the value of the income itself, that counts. In terms of our candle and disk illustration, it is a factor affecting the size of the disk, rather than a factor affecting the distance between the disk and the candle. For the purposes of calculation, the two elements in the nominal rate of interest may be lumped together, and the nominal rate, rather than the pure rate, may be taken as the rate of discount for capitalization purposes. But for theoretical purposes, the two must be kept distinct. The capitalization theory rests on the assumption of a fixed value of the money unit.

That the fixed value of the money unit assumed is an absolute value, and not a mere "reciprocal of the price level," may be proved by some further considerations regarding relations among these same factors. Assume a fall in the rate of interest. Then, on the capitalization theory, prices of lands, stocks and bonds, houses, horses, and all items of wealth which give forth their services through an appreciable period of time, will rise, and with them the average of prices, or the general price level, will rise.[60] If one hold the *relative* conception of value, according to which the value of money necessarily falls when prices rise, because the two are merely obverse phases of the same thing, then this rise in the price level is, *ipso facto*, a fall in the value of money. But we have seen that a fall in the value of money means, on the "principle of appreciation and interest," a rise in the interest rate! Hence, we would have proved that a fall in the interest rate causes a rise in the interest rate—which is absurd. If, however, we recognize that prices can rise without a fall in the value of money, if, *i. e.*, we use the absolute conception of value, this difficulty disappears. The capitalization theory and the theory of appreciation and interest can be reconciled only on the basis of the absolute conception of value.

The capitalization theory, then, in its present formulation, assumes money, and a fixed absolute value of money. It is, therefore, inapplicable to the problem of the value of money itself.

In general, none of the polished tools of the economic analysis,—neither cost of production, the capitalization theory,[61] nor the law of supply and demand,—is applicable to the problem of the value of money. The reason is that they get their edge from money itself. The razor does not easily cut the hone. It is to this fact, I think, that we owe the widespread and long continued vogue of a theory so crude and mechanical as the quantity theory. In the next chapter we shall show that the utility theory of value—which we shall not recognize as a polished tool!—has also failed to give us help in explaining the value of money.

CHAPTER V

MARGINAL UTILITY AND THE VALUE OF MONEY

A good many writers have attempted to apply the marginal utility theory to the value of money. Among these, I may particularly mention Friedrich Wieser, Ludwig von Mises, Joseph Schumpeter, and, in America, David Kinley, and H. J. Davenport.

The marginal utility theory is ordinarily merely a thinly disguised version of supply and demand doctrine. As usually presented in the text-books, we have an analysis of the phenomenon of diminishing utility of a given commodity to a given individual, illustrated by a diagram, in which the ordinates represent diminishing psychological intensities. Often a money measure is given to these diminishing intensities, and the curve is presented as the demand schedule of a given individual. Then, with little further analysis, a leap is made to the market, and it is assumed that the market demand-curve, of many individuals, differing in wealth and character, is a utility-curve, and value in the market is "explained" by means of marginal utility. I need not here repeat my criticisms of this procedure.[62] It gives simply a confused statement of the doctrine of supply and demand. The analysis of utility which precedes the discussion of market demand is wholly irrelevant, and merely mixes things up. That such a conception is of no use in solving the problem of the value of money has been sufficiently indicated in the chapter on supply and demand.

Sometimes the contention is made that money is unique among goods in having "no power to satisfy human wants except a power *to purchase* things which do have such power."[63] This contention, in Professor Fisher's view, precludes the application of the marginal utility theory to the problem of the value of money, and he makes no use of marginal utility in his explanation. Indeed, in the passage from which this quotation is taken, Professor Fisher says that the quantity theory of money rests on just this peculiarity of money. Not all writers who contend that money has no utility *per se*, however, have felt it necessary to give up the marginal utility theory as a theory of money, as we shall later see.

On the other hand, writers of the "commodity school" (or "metallist school"), writers who see the source of the value of money in the metal of which it is made, can apply the utility theory readily to the value of money, making the value of money depend on the marginal utility of gold, or the standard metal, whatever it is. To the writers of this school, it is incredible that anything which has no utility should become money. Money must be either valuable itself, or else a representative of some valuable thing. The value of money comes from the value of the standard of value, and that value may, so far as the logic of the situation is concerned, be as well explained by marginal utility as the value of anything else. Typical of this view is Professor W. A. Scott's discussion in his *Money and Banking*[64], though the emphasis there is not on marginal utility as the explanation of the value of the standard, but on the value (conceived of as an absolute quantity) of the standard as essential to the existence of money, and the performance of the money functions. Professor Scott attacks vigorously and effectively Nicholson's exposition of the quantity theory,[65] where the assumption is made that money consists of dodo-bones (the most useless thing Nicholson could think of). Most quantity theorists would share Nicholson's view that dodo-bones would serve as well as anything else for money—or, to put the thing less fantastically, that the substance of which money is made is irrelevant, that the only question is as to the quantity, rather than the quality, of the money-units, and the quantity of the money-units, not in pounds or bushels or yards, but in abstract number merely. For writers who seek the whole explanation of the value of money in its monetary application, and who see that money, *qua* money, cannot administer directly to human wants, the view that Professor Fisher expresses, namely, that money has no utility, and is unique among goods in this respect, seems on the surface, to have justification. On the surface merely, however. Money is not unique among goods in being wanted only for what it can be traded for. Wheat and corn and stocks and bonds and everything else that is speculated in is wanted, by the speculators, only as a means of getting a profit[66]—they are remoter from the wants of the man who purchases them than the money profit he anticipates. Ginsing, in America, has value, though consumed only in China. And there are people, particularly jewelers, who often want money as a raw material for consumption goods. The difference is at most a difference of degree—and of slight degree indeed in the case of such things as bonds, which count on the "goods" side of the quantity theory price equation, but which really are in all cases remoter than money itself from human wants. Money really stands, for the purpose in hand, on the same level as any other instrumental good.[67] It does not give forth services directly, as a rule. Neither does a machine, or an acre of wheat land, or goods in a wholesaler's warehouse. Exchange is a productive process, an essential part of the present process of production. Money is a tool which enormously facilitates this process. It has its peculiarities, no doubt. One of them is—and money is not unique in this as will later appear—that it must have *value* from non-monetary sources[68] before it can perform its own special functions, from some of which it draws an increased value. But there seems to me to be nothing in the contention quoted from Professor Fisher, to justify setting money sharply off from all other things, or to justify the view that marginal utility is inapplicable to the value of money, if it be applicable to the value of anything at all that is not destined for immediate consumption. I do not believe that the marginal utility theory is valid for any class of goods, not even those for immediate consumption. Where marginal utility theory is,—as in the conventional text-book expositions—merely another name for supply and demand theory, it is, as already shown, not applicable to the value of money, and it is useful in the surface explanation of market-prices of goods. But where marginal utility theory really seeks to get at value fundamentals, it is precisely as valid for money as for goods of other sorts—invalid, in my judgment, in both places, and for the same reasons in both.

Among the writers who would apply the utility theory to money, while still insisting that money, as such, has no utility, are Wieser, Schumpeter—who accepts Wieser's theory in its main outlines—and von Mises, who develops a notion very different from that of the other two.

Wieser's doctrines are set forth in two expositions, separated by five years, the second representing a considerable development in his thought, though resting in part on the first. The first is an address upon the occasion of his accession to the professorship at the University of Vienna, in 1904, and is published in the *Zeitschrift für Volkswirtschaft, Sozialpolitik und Verwaltung*, vol. 13 entitled, "Der Geldwert und seine geschichtlichen Veränderungen." The second is a discussion, partly written and partly spoken, "Der Geldwert und seine Veränderungen" (written), and "Ueber die Messung der Veränderungen des Geldwertes" (spoken), in *Schriften des Vereins für Sozialpolitik, Referate zur Tagung*, no. 132, 1909. For the purpose in hand, a brief statement of one or two points would suffice to show the futility of Wieser's effort to get an explanation of the value of money *via* marginal utility, but I think that readers may be interested in a fuller account of Wieser's doctrine, just because it is Wieser's, and so shall undertake to give a more systematic account of it. For brevity, in the exposition which follows, I shall refer to the first article as "I," and to the second as "II."[69]

Wieser holds that it is possible to have money wholly apart from a commodity basis (I, p. 45), citing the Austrian *Staatsnoten* as a case in point. The reason for giving them up is that they do not circulate in foreign trade. Gold fulfills its international money-functions the more easily because of its various employments, but, after it is thoroughly historically introduced, as money, it could fulfill its money functions even if all these employments be thought away (46). Wieser gives no argument for this contention, and its validity will be examined later.[70] There are, he says, two sources for the value of gold, the money use and the arts use, interacting. Money is further removed from wants, not only than consumption goods, but also than production goods, which are but consumption goods in the seed. The latter are technically destined for definite goods. But money may be used to procure whatever good you please, in exchange. (The absoluteness of this distinction, also, may be questioned. Pig iron is almost as unspecialized as money in its relation to wants, since tools enter into the production of almost every service that human wants require, from surgical operations, through instrumental music, to wheat and horse-shoes. On the other hand, money is not the only thing by means of which other things are purchased. The extent of barter in modern life will wait for later discussion.[71] I do not think that *any* sharp distinction between money and all other things is valid.) Wieser complains of the older economics which treats money as a commodity. And he contends that as money and commodities show a contrast in their essence (*Wesen*), they should also manifest a contrast in the laws of their values, even though the fundamental general theory of value applies to both (I, 47). He finds in representatives of money (*Geldsurrogate*) and in velocity of circulation of money, factors which are lacking in commodities. (Again a question must be interjected by the writer. Are not corporation securities essentially like *Geldsurrogate* from this angle? And do not goods vary greatly in the number of times they are exchanged? What of the speculative markets, where more sales are made in an active market, at times, than there are commodities or securities of the type dealt in in existence?) The value of money is essentially bound up with the money-service. Wieser indicates that he is not talking about the subjective value of money, but its objective value, using the popular meaning of the term, which, he says, is not strictly logical, but is useful: the relation of money to all other goods which are exchanged, the purchasing power of money. This depends on goods as well as on money. In the second article, Wieser refines and elaborates his conception of the objective value of money, seeking to get away from the notion of relativity which is involved in the conception of purchasing power, and to get an absolute conception, which shall be a causal factor in the determination of general prices, rather than a mere reflection of them. It is to be a coefficient with the objective values of goods in determining prices. A change in general prices may be caused by a change in the value of money, and may be caused by a change in the values of goods (II, p. 511). In explaining this objective value concept (which, in its formal and logical aspects, is in many ways similar to the absolute social value concept maintained by the present writer, though, in the present writer's judgment, inadequately accounted for by Wieser, so far as a psychological causal theory is concerned) Wieser objects to the term, "objective value" which he had used in the earlier article. He prefers "volkswirtschaftlicher Wert." (This term is perhaps best rendered "public economic value," for present purposes, to distinguish it, on the one hand, from individual or personal value, and, on the other, from the social economic value concept of the present writer. At the same time, the connotation of a communistic or authoritive value must not be read into the term. It is, in its formal and logical aspects, really the most common of all the value notions, and may, best of all perhaps, be translated simply "value," or "economic value," or "absolute value." But for the present discussion, we shall call it "public economic value.") This public economic value, in the case of goods, is not a mere objective relation between a good and its price-equivalent. It is a subjective (psychological) value, like personal value. If one wishes to call it objective value, one is using objective in the sense of the general subjective as distinguished from the personal individual idiosyncracy (II, p. 502). The objective exchange value of goods (here Wieser uses "objektiver Tauschwert" as the equivalent of his "volkswirtschaftlicher Wert" above mentioned) is the common subjective part of the individual valuations leaving out the remainder of individual peculiarities ("der allgemein subjective Teil der persönlichen Wertschätzungen mit Verschweigung des individual eigenartig empfundenen Restes").[72] Wieser does not seem to me to think out clearly the distinction between absolute and relative value in this connection. He wishes to get something more fundamental than a mere relation between goods and money; he wishes a psychological phenomenon. He wishes to have a value of goods which can be set over against the value of money, the two, in combination, determining prices. And yet, he wishes somehow to get these out of the prices themselves. "We must seek a concept of the public economic value of money which, to be sure, proceeds from the general price-level (*Preisstand*), but which excludes from its content everything that comes purely from the value of goods" (II,

511). To the public economic value of money, however, Wieser gives no independent definition. The definition runs in terms of the values of the goods. "The value of money rises when the same inner values (*innere Werte*) of commodities are expressed in lower prices; it falls, when they are expressed in higher prices" (II, 511-12). "Inner value" of goods is not defined, but I take it that Wieser uses it as meaning essentially the same thing as the public economic value already described—an absolute value. (*Cf.* the usage of Menger and von Mises, *infra*, in this chapter, with respect to the terms, "inner" and "outer" value.) The definition is not strictly circular, perhaps, but at least it is pretty empty. Nothing appears to give the value of money, as distinct from its purchasing power, an independent standing. The reason for this will later appear. It should be noted, however, that the definition is not in terms of prices or purchasing power. Prices might remain unchanged, in Wieser's scheme, and yet the value of money sink, if the inner values of goods should sink.

The value of money, thus defined, is to be explained by marginal utility. But money has no marginal utility of its own, it has no subjective use-value, but only a subjective exchange value,—derived from the use-value (marginal utility) of the commodity purchased with the marginal dollar (II, 507-8). This subjective-exchange value of money is the personal value of money, as distinguished from its public economic value, and is the cause of the public economic value. The personal value of money changes (1) with the volume of one's personal income, (2) with the intensity of one's need for money, and (3) with market prices. The personal value of money is directly influenced and measured only in exchanges for consumption goods. Expenditures of other kinds affect it only indirectly by leaving less for consumption expenditures. The laborer always reckons with the personal value of money, but not the business man, in his business calculations. As in the case of goods, we pass from personal to public economic value (II, 509). The personal value of money depends on the relation between an individual's money income, and his real income, in terms of goods. The public economic value of money depends on the money income of the community as a whole, and its real income. (II, 516-18). Money income grows faster than real income, through the extension of the money economy. Money income is not, like real income, dependent on quantity. The mere extension of the money economy increases the volume of money income, lowers the personal value of money, lowers its public economic value, and raises prices. Witness the effect on a rural community of bringing it into the great market, where all costs are reckoned in money and rising costs compel rising prices. Hence, there is a tendency for the public economic value of money to sink, and this has been the historical fact (I, II, 519-520.)

Criticism of this theory is almost superfluous. There are elements in Wieser's discussion, not here presented, which have very considerable importance, and which will be presented in a later chapter when the criticism of the quantity theory is taken up. Wieser deals some heavy blows to the quantity theory. But his constructive doctrine presents the clearest possible case of the Austrian circle. The value of money depends, not on its subjective use-value, its own marginal utility—it has none. The value of money depends on its subjective value in exchange, the marginal utility of the goods which are exchanged for it. But these depend on prices. And prices depend, in part, on the value of money itself! This circle, present in every form of the Austrian theory which seeks a causal explanation of value and prices by means of marginal utility,[73] though often less obviously present, is here quite glaring. The distinction between volume of money income and quantity of money is, on the other hand, an important one, and will be emphasized when the quantity theory is taken up.[74] One further point in Wieser's doctrine calls for comment. It is strange indeed to find an Austrian seeing in a rise in money costs a *cause* of a general rise in prices. The Austrian doctrine is rather that rising money costs are *reflections* of rising general prices. Wieser's doctrine that the extension of the money economy to rural regions, compelling the farmer to reckon all his costs in money and so to raise his prices, has been adequately criticised by von Mises, who points out that Wieser sees only half the phenomenon; that eggs and butter are, indeed, higher in price in the rural region when it comes into contact with the city, but that they are correspondingly lower in the city from the same cause. On the other hand, the doctrine of costs is not the whole point in Wieser's notion of the extension of the money economy as a cause of higher prices, and we shall deal with the doctrine again, in a different connection.

By devitalizing the marginal utility theory, by stating it in such a way that it makes no causal assertions, and in such a way that it leaves the real value problem untouched, it is possible to free it from the circle just pointed out. Schumpeter does so state it.

Schumpeter's theory of value,[75] though he attributes it to Böhm-Bawerk, seems to the present writer to be essentially different. Böhm-Bawerk undertakes to explain the value (objective value in exchange) of each good by its *own* marginal utility to different individuals, buyers and sellers of the good—indeed, by its marginal utility to *four* individuals, the two "marginal pairs."[76] He sees at points that the prices of other goods are sometimes factors, making marginal utility give way to "subjective value in exchange," as the determinant of an individual's behavior toward a given good in the market—as in his much discussed overcoat illustration.[77] But Böhm-Bawerk never gets out of the circle which this reaction of the market-prices on the individual subjective values involves. Schumpeter seems to rise to a higher conspectus picture, which, in form, avoids the circle. His picture is that of a vast equilibrium, in which, instead of attributing the market value of each good to its own marginal utility, you explain the exchange ratios[78] of every good to every other good, all at once, by reference to a total situation: *given* the number of goods of each class, given the number of individuals in the market, given the *distribution* of each class of goods among the individuals, given the utility-*curves* (not marginal utilities) of each good to each individual, an equilibrium will be reached, through trading, in which ratios between marginal utilities of each kind of good to each individual are inversely proportional to the abstract ratios (ratios of exchange) between the same goods, each measured in its own unit. The ratios are abstract ratios, between pure numbers, so far as the market ratios are concerned; the ratios in the mind of each individual are concrete ratios, between marginal utilities. The scheme, thus stated, says nothing as to the *causal* relation between marginal utility and market ratios; it merely states certain *mathematical* relations between each individual system of marginal utilities on the one hand, and the abstract market ratios on the other. By avoiding *assertions* as to causation, it avoids a causal circle. In such a situation, marginal utilities and market ratios are, in reality, alike resultants, *effects*, of the given quantities of goods, distribution of goods, numbers of buyers and sellers, and individual utility-curves—not *marginal* utilities. To this picture, one may add—what Schumpeter does not add—the curves showing time-preferences of each individual for each sort of good, and (an element which Schumpeter does include) the curves of *dis*-utility for the individuals who produce each kind of good. The system, it may be noted, is as good a proof of *real cost* doctrine as it is of utility doctrine.

Such a picture, I submit, avoids the circle which is presented in all other formulations of the Austrian theory of value. I wish, however, to indicate its limitations as a theory of value, and the impossibility of any application of it to the problem of the value of money. (1) Its data are inaccessible: nobody could possibly know all the utility-curves and all the time-preference curves (and disutility of labor-curves, etc.) of all goods to all individuals in, say, the United States. To explain market ratios by utility-curves is a case of *ignotum per ignotius,* so far as practical application is concerned. Moreover, the scheme is so difficult to visualize that it is useless as a tool of thought— as one will find who tries to think it through, without the aid of higher mathematics, for ten goods, and ten persons, with unequal distribution of wealth, and different utility curves, time-preference curves, and disutility-curves for each kind of good to each individual. (2) The scheme must assume smooth curves and infinitesimal increments in consumption, which is a fiction so far as the individual psychology is concerned. Without this assumption, the point-for-point correspondence between individual and market ratios does not exist. It is only in social-value curves, or in demand-curves in the big market (which are social-value curves, expressed in money),[79] that you have, as a matter of fact, the right to smooth out your curves. (3) The theory must assume the frictionless static state, in which marginal adjustments are perfectly accomplished, and equilibrium really reached. Without this assumption, again the point-for-point inverse correspondence of market ratios and individual ratios fails. But this makes it quite impossible to apply the doctrine to any functional theory of the value of money, or to bring money in any realistic way into the scheme. As will be shown more fully in later chapters, money functions in bringing about just the absence of friction which static theory assumes. That is what money is *for*. The functional theory of money, therefore, cannot abstract from friction and dynamic change.[80] It is, of course, possible, on this scheme to pick out any one of the goods in the system, say the 1-1000th part of a horse, call it the "money-unit," and determine a set of money-prices. These "money-prices" are already given in the scheme in the ratios between the abstract numbers of this unit and the abstract numbers of the units of all other goods. But this is meaningless, so far as a theory of money is concerned. It abstracts entirely from the *differences* in *salability*[81] of goods, on which the theory of money must rest. It gives us no clue to that part of the value of the money-article which comes from its money-functions.

(4) The theory has no bearing on the problems of supply and demand. Demand-curves are curves, not of utility, but of money-prices. They are concerned, not with a *system* of ratios among goods in general, but with the absolute money-prices of particular goods, one at a time. The modern demand-curves and supply-curves, representing the demand and supply doctrine first made precise by J. S. Mill,[82] are concerned with the money-prices of particular goods, and the "equation of supply and demand"—amount supplied and amount demanded—gives an equilibrium in which only one price is determined. Austrian theory, in Böhm-Bawerk's hands, and in the hands of practically all adherents of the Austrian School, including Davenport,[83] has been offered as really bearing on the explanation of demand, and as giving a psychological account and explanation of the demand-curve. The scheme of Schumpeter has simply no bearing at all on this vital point. The equilibrium picture in which *all* goods are involved supplies no data from which to construct any of the magnitudes above or below the margin of the demand and supply-curves of any given good. One reason why this is so will appear from the point made with reference to "money-prices" in the preceding paragraph. For Schumpeter's scheme, the significance of the article chosen as "money" would be as much a problem as anything else, when the conditions are laid down. It would vary in the process of reaching the equilibrium. Its ratios with all other things would, thus, fluctuate until the equilibrium was reached. But, as we have seen, in the chapter on "Supply and Demand," curves of supply and demand must assume a fixed significance of the money-unit. It may be further noticed, as marking off Schumpeter's scheme from supply and demand analysis, that in Schumpeter's scheme, the individual is the centre of interest, and his reactions *toward all kinds of goods* is emphasized; whereas in supply and demand analysis, the *good*—one good—is the centre of interest, and the price-offers streaming toward it from all kinds of individuals is emphasized. The two bodies of doctrine are quite distinct.

(5) The theory has no bearing on the explanation of entrepreneur cost—money-outlay, "opportunity cost," alternative positive values, or what not. It finds no place for the modern cost doctrine. It does not in any way open the path to the Austrian theory of costs. Costs, for Austrian theory, as, in general, for modern theory, are reflections of *demand* for the employment of the agents of production in alternative uses. Thus, it costs a great deal to raise wheat in Illinois, because of the rival demand for the land to produce corn. Labor costs are high in ordinary manufacturing, because of the rival demand for labor in the munitions factories, etc. As Schumpeter's theory can give no account of the *demand* for labor in the munitions factories, it follows that it can give no account of the *cost* of labor in the other factories. Instead, indeed, of giving us the modern cost doctrine, we see Schumpeter's scheme reviving the old *real cost* doctrine, running in terms of sacrifices in production.[84]

(6) The foregoing paragraph gives emphasis to the point with which we started, namely, that Schumpeter's theory is not a *causal* theory, but merely a theory which gives mathematical relations in a static picture. For the general theory of the Austrians, this real cost doctrine is anathema. Values are positive. The emphasis is put on positive wants, as *causes* which guide and motivate industry. The *clue* to all values is in the values of *consumption* goods, which are in direct contact with the utilities which are the source of value. From the values of consumption goods, we *derive* the values of production goods, labor, etc., which are goods of "second, third and fourth *ranks*" and whose values are merely reflected from the causal marginal utilities of the consumption goods they are destined to create. None of this causation is brought into Schumpeter's conspectus picture. On the contrary, with the bringing in of disutility of production, we have the doctrine of the earlier English School revived. The equilibrium picture is as good a proof of the one theory as of the other. If we assume the utility-curves constant, and allow the cost-curves to vary, then causation would be initiated by the cost-curves.[85]

(7) Such an equilibrium picture leaves untouched the vital question which any theory must answer which means to be of practical use in concrete situations: what are the real *variables* in the situation, and what factors are constant? What causes are *likely* to produce changes in market prices? The individual-utility curves, which in Austrian theory are commonly treated as

the only variables, except quantities of goods,—in the strict static picture there are no variables at all!—are really, when conceived of as individual, as growing out of the mental processes of each individual separately, the most *constant* factor in the situation. For, on the principle of the inertia of large numbers, each unit of which is moved by its own peculiar causes, changes in the utility-curves of one man will be offset by opposite changes in the utility-curves of another, and so the general system will remain much where it was. Of course, if a rich man changes his curve, a poor man's change will not offset it in the market, but this is to emphasize the *distribution of wealth* rather than the utility-curves. It is only when you get changes of a sort that the individualistic psychology, and the "pure economic" explanation factors, of the Austrians find no place for, that you can predict a change in the general price-system. It is only changes in fashion or mode, in general business confidence,[86] in moral attitude toward this or the other sort of consumption or production, in the distribution of wealth, changes in taxes and other laws—causes of a general social character—that you can count on to produce important changes in values. Of course, changes in the adequacies of supplies would be taken account of on either interpretation.

(8) The scheme under consideration gives no value concept which the economist can make any particular use of. It gives only ratios between marginal utilities in the mind of the same individual, and abstract market ratios. It gives no *quantitative* value, which can be attributed to goods as a quality,[87] a homogeneous quality of wealth by means of which diverse sorts of wealth may be compared, funded, etc. Such a concept is, however, necessary for the economic analysis, and Schumpeter is driven to creating substitutes for it of various sorts, notably *Kaufkraft* and *Kapital*. *Kaufkraft*, as Schumpeter uses the term, is not derived from marginal utility, but is an abstraction from the idea of money. It is not a quantity of money alone, nor even of money and credit, but is a fund of "abstract power," which depends not alone on the quantity of money and credit in which it is embodied, but also on the prices of goods.[88] This *Kaufkraft* is needed to give the causal "steam," the "motivating power," which the social value concept connotes, but which ratios in the market lack. Similarly, *Kapital* is conceived of as an agent, a dynamic force, distinguished from accumulations of concrete productive instruments, by means of which the entrepreneur gets control of

land, labor and instrumental goods.[89] Other functions of the quantitative value are shouldered on a hard-worked and unusually defined concept, *Kredit*, which leads Schumpeter into certain "heresies"[90] regarding credit, which are mostly harmless in themselves, but which will arouse misunderstanding and opposition. "*Præter necessitatem entia non multiplicanda sunt*," and the social value concept, which covers by inclusion the notion of market ratio—market ratios being ratios between social values—and which does all the work that Schumpeter attributes to *Kapital* and *Kaufkraft*, and most of the new work which he attributes to *Kredit*, is to be preferred,[91] if only on grounds of intellectual economy. "Capital" is then saved for more usual meanings, and economy in terminology is also effected. Schumpeter also departs, as shown, from the abstract market ratio notion in erecting a causal theory of value, in which "marginal utility" is used as the equivalent of a quantitative value, and is traced by the Austrian imputation process back to the original factors of production. He even speaks of labor as having "utility," whereas labor,[92] unless used in domestic service, has, not utility, but only value.

In the marginal utility scheme above outlined there is no place for money, on the assumptions laid down. It is a scheme of barter relations. The utilities which come into equilibrium are not subjective-exchange-values, which, as Schumpeter, with Wieser, contends, are the only subjective values money has, but are real subjective use values—marginal utilities. The scheme, assuming as it does, perfect exchangeability of all goods, with infinitesimal increments in consumption, has no place for money. There really is no money service to be performed. Schumpeter, indeed, speaks of money as a mere "Schleier," which does not touch the essence of the phenomena, and such it is on his assumptions. In a similar situation, Professor Irving Fisher gives up the effort to find a psychological explanation of the value of money,[93] and offers the quantity theory as a mechanical principle, additional to the psychological barter scheme. Schumpeter, however, does lip service still to the need for a psychological explanation. His answer runs in Wieser's terms—indeed, he attributes it to Wieser. The *Preis* of money[94] —Schumpeter does not use Wieser's absolute value concept, but lets his value of money run in purely relative terms—the price of money in goods depends on the subjective value of money. This subjective value of money rests on the experience of each individual in making purchases—rests on the prices of consumption goods, determined by the relation between real income and money income. The circle is as clear as day.

Ludwig von Mises sees this circle, and tries to avoid it. In von Mises there seem to me to be very noteworthy clarity and power. His *Theorie des Geldes und der Umlaufsmittel* is an exceptionally excellent book. Von Mises has a very wide knowledge of the literature of the theory of money. He has a keen insight into the difficulties involved. He recognizes fully that, so far, the utility school has failed to solve the problem (119-120). His theory is as follows: Individual valuations (93) constitute the basis of the objective exchange value of money. But while for other goods, subjective use-value and subjective exchange-value are different concepts, for money the two coincide, and both rest on the objective value of money (94). This seems to be our old circle in unmistakable form, but Mises thinks he has an escape, as will later appear. No function of money is thinkable which does not rest on its objective exchange value. The subjective value of money rests on the subjective use-values of the goods for which it can be exchanged (95). Money, at the beginning of its money-functioning, must have objective exchange value from other causes than its money-function, but it can remain valuable, even though these causes fall away, exclusively through its function as general instrument of exchange (111). He gives no argument in support of this contention, but refers with approval to Wieser (*loc. cit.*), and to Simmel (*Philosophie des Geldes*, 115ff.). Hence, the important consequence that in the value of money of to-day a historical component is contained. Herein is to be found a fundamental contrast between the value of money and the values of other goods (119-120.). The individual valuation of money rests on the objective exchange value of money of *yesterday*. This individual value of money is the explanation, on the money side, of the objective value of money of to-day. Going back, step by step, you come ultimately to the subjective use-value of the money-stuff in its non-monetary employment—a temporal *regressus*. This opens the way to a theory of the value of money based on marginal utility. This avoids the circle of explaining the objective value of money of to-day by the subjective exchange value of money of to-day, which in turn rests on the contemporary objective value of money.

I find this particularly interesting, since it employs a device which had once suggested itself to me as a means of escape from the Austrian circle, but which reflection led me to abandon. I have discussed the whole matter in my *Social Value*, and therefore venture a quotation from that book.[95]

"How are we to get out of our circle:[96] The value of a good, A, depends, in part, upon the value embodied in the goods, B, C, and D, possessed by the persons for whom good A has 'utility,' and whose 'effective demand' is a *sine qua non* of A's value? The most convenient point of departure seems to be the simple situation which Wieser has assumed in his *Natural Value*.[97] Here the 'artificial' complications due to private property and to the difference between rich and poor are gone, and only 'marginal utility' is left as a regulator of values. But what about value in a situation where there are differences in 'purchasing power'? How assimilate the one situation to the other?

"A *temporal regressus*, back to the first piece of wealth, which, we might assume, depended for its value solely upon the facts of utility and scarcity, and the existence of which furnished the first 'purchasing power' that upset the order of 'natural value,' might be interesting, but certainly would not be convincing. In the first place, there is no unbroken sequence of uninterrupted economic causation from that far away hypothetical day to the present, in the course of which that original quantity of value has exerted its influence. The present situation does not differ from Wieser's situation simply in the fact that some, more provident than others, have saved where others have consumed, have been industrious where others have been idle, and so have accumulated a surplus of value, which, used to back their desires, makes the wants of the industrious and provident count for more than the wants of others. And even if these were the only differences, it is to be noted that private property has somehow crept in in the interval, for Wieser's was a communistic society. And further, an emotion felt ten thousand years ago could scarcely have any very direct or certain quantitative connection with value in the market to-day. Even if there had been no 'disturbing factors' of a non-economic sort, the process of 'economic causation' could not have carried a value so far. It is the living emotion that counts! Values depend every moment upon the force of live minds, and need to be constantly renewed. And there would have been, of course, many 'non-economic' disturbances, wars and robberies, frauds and benevolences, political and religious changes—a host of historical occurrences affecting the weight of different elements in society in a way that, by historical methods, it is impossible to treat quantitatively.[98]

"What is called for is, not a temporal *regressus*, which, starting with an hypothesis, picks up abstractions by the way, and tries to synthesize them into a concrete reality of to-day, but rather, a *logical analysis* of existing psychic forces, which shall abstract from the concrete social situation the phases that are most significant. This method will not give us the whole story either. Value will not be completely explained by the phases we pick out. But then, we shall be aware of the fact, and we shall know that the other phases are there, ready to be picked out as they are needed for further refinement of the theory, as new problems call for further refinement. And, indeed, we shall include them in our theory, under a lump name, namely, the rest of the 'presuppositions' of value.

"Our reason for choosing a logical analysis of existing psychic forces instead of a temporal *regressus*—instead, even, of an accurate historical study of the past—is a two-fold one: first, we wish to coördinate the new factors we are to emphasize with factors already recognized, and to emerge with a value concept which shall serve the economists in the accustomed way—it is illogical to mix a logical analysis with a temporal *regressus*. But, more fundamental than this logical point, is this: the forces which have historically *begot* a social situation are not, necessarily, the forces which *sustain* it. The rule doubtless is that new institutions have to win their way against an opposition which grows simply out of the fact that we are, through mental inertia, wedded to what is old and familiar. We resist the new *as* the new. Even those who are most disposed to innovate are still conservative, with reference to propaganda that they themselves are not concerned with. The great mass of activities of all men, even the most progressive, are rooted in habit, and resist change. When, however, a new value has won its way, has become familiar and established, the very forces which once opposed it now become its surest support. Or, waiving this unreflecting inertia of society, as things become actualized they are seen in new relations. What, prior to experiment, we thought might harm us, we find beneficial after it has been tried, and so support it—or the reverse may be true. The psychic forces maintaining and controlling a social situation, therefore, are not necessarily the ones which historically brought it into being."[99]

Since the foregoing was written, I have found that another theorist, Professor Alvin S. Johnson, had also given consideration to the same idea, as a means of escape from the Austrian circle. Professor Johnson refers to the notion briefly in his review of *Social Value* (*Am. Econ. Rev.*, June, 1912, p. 322), holding that the doctrine is logically tenable, though rejecting it on psychological grounds. "The value of a thing newly created can be explained only with reference to values antecedently existing." That there is a continuity in the value system, as in the whole social-mental life of men, I should be the last to deny. But it is not the antecedently existing values, *as* antecedently existing, that give value to the new piece of wealth. The antecedent values function only as *persisting*, as *contemporary* social forces. We do not find the motivating power of existing values in the ashes of burnt out desire! It seems to me very essential to distinguish the two methods of approach to the problem. It is possible to state a historical sequence—if you know it,—showing how values have historically come and gone. But for an equilibrium picture, of the sort that our price theory demands, where there is a mechanical balancing of contemporary factors (as in Marshall's balls in the bowl illustration), such an account is of no use. Existing social forces have their history. But, at a given moment, they are what they are, and what they *were* at a different time adds no ounce of weight to the power they now exert. If a quantitative account of value is called for—and price-theory is essentially concerned with the measurement of values—we must bring measure and measured into contemporary balance. The historical account is one thing; the cross-section analysis is another. "Static theory" is a mechanical abstraction from the organic cross-section picture, which, by making it superficial, is able to make it exact.

It seems to me that this distinction must be kept clear if progress in the science is to be made. At every point, divergent conclusions are reached if the two view-points are merged. The distinction between statics and dynamics is, in a general way, the same as the distinction here made between the historical and the cross-section view. It is no answer to the Ricardian theory of land-rent for Carey to point out that historically, in new countries, the uplands are cultivated first, and the more fertile river-valleys later. Ricardo is talking about statics, and Carey about dynamics. Carey does not answer Ricardo, because he is talking about a different problem. The utility theorist especially has no right to leave the static view-point. All the elementary laws on which the utility theory is based are static laws. The law of satiety, of diminishing utility, is a static law, and the utility theorists are careful to point out that it holds only for an individual at a given time. It rests on nerve fatigue. Give the nerve time to rest, and utility does not sink. On the contrary, the dynamic law of wants is that wants expand. As old wants are satisfied, new wants arise, so that, in the course of time, *marginal* utilities do not sink—the competition of new wants forces up the margins of the old wants. Moreover, with time, tastes change, habits are formed, and the same wants may grow more intense—as in the case of olives or whiskey. All this has been seen by the creators of the utility theory. Thus, Wieser: "The want as a whole of course retains its strength so long as a man retains his health; satisfaction does not weaken but rather stimulates it, by constantly contributing to its development, and, particularly, by giving rise to a desire for variety. It is otherwise with the separate sensations of the want. These are narrowly limited both in point of time and in point of matter. Anyone who has just taken a certain quantity of food of a certain kind will not immediately have the same strength of desire for a similar quantity. Within any single period of want every additional act of satisfaction will be estimated less highly than a preceding one obtained from a quantity of goods equal in kind and amount." (*Natural Value*, p. 9.) A similar statement is in Taussig's *Principles* (I, 124), "In such cases, however, the tastes of the purchasers may be said to have changed in the interval. At any given stage of taste and popularity, the principle of diminishing utility will apply." Illustrations could be multiplied.

It is true that *future* marginal utilities come into the utility theory scheme, but they come in, not as future utilities, but as "*present worths*" of future utilities, or as "present anticipated feelings" in Jevons' phrase[100] suffering a discount, usually, in the process. But I am not aware of any writer among the founders of the utility school, who has sought to bring past utilities into the scheme. The past is dead. Its effects persist in the present only in present processes. A *memory* is a *present* psychological fact.

Consider further. Is it the prices of yesterday that determine the subjective value of money to an individual, if the prices of yesterday are different from the prices of to-day, *and the individual knows it*? In so far as we have the clear, intelligent economic mind, seeking its interests—and the marginal utility theory assumes this type of mind—the tendency is to bring all the factors in the problem into the present. If prices change slowly, so that the individual can count on essentially the same situation to-day that he had yesterday, doubtless he will not take the trouble to recast his value system. There is a tremendous lot of trouble in bringing about, in the individual's mind, the rational equilibration of values—trouble which the Austrian theory commonly abstracts from, but which should be recognized in the analysis, and accorded its own marginal significance in the scale. To throw the emphasis on inertia, however, and to assume that men do not readjust their margins to meet changed conditions, is to depart from the fundamentals of the Austrian theory. If the price-situation is a rapidly changing one, men do rapidly readjust their estimates of money. If money is fluctuating rapidly in value—as, say, during a time when there is depreciated paper money, whose future depends on military events, the adjustments may be very rapid indeed. I quote the following from the news columns of the *New York Times*, of April 4, 1914, p. 2: "Jaurez, Mexico, Apr. 3.—After the hysterical outbursts last night that greeted the news of the fall of Torreon, this city was preternaturally calm to-day.... The silent gentleman with the dyed mustache who spins the marble at the roulette wheel in the Jaurez Monte Carlo, conducted by Villa's officers for the benefit of the rebel treasury, seemed the only person who was not excited. When the crowd of players suddenly deserted him on the sound of the bugle call of victory, he gave the marble another whirl from sheer force of habit, but none returned.... In an hour, however, play was faster and more furious than ever, for holders of Constitutionalist money early realized that their currency had suddenly increased in value, and that they were somewhat richer than before." I do not question the fact, however, that men are slow in making calculations, and that society is often unconscious of changed conditions, and often readjusts less rapidly than occasion requires. There is a vast deal of inertia, of blind habit, of custom, etc. But emphasis on these factors is not marginal utility theory! Factors like these are emphasized by a functional psychology, and by a social psychology—not by an individualistic psychology which rests on the assumption of rational calculation. It is not *past* utilities that explain present subjective values of money when these subjective values are out of harmony with the present market facts, but rather *present* habits, present customs, present disinclination to readjust, etc. There is a big difference, psychologically, between the mental processes through which one arrived at one's present state of mind, and the present state of mind itself. The original "commodity utility" of the money metal, in the far away time before the money use affected its value, is surely no longer a factor. Certainly not on the basis of an individualistic psychology of the Austrian type. All the individuals who experienced that original utility are long since dead! Not even memories of the original utilities persist.

When writing the passage in *Social Value*, quoted above, I did not suppose that I was dealing with a notion that anyone else would ever take seriously. My purpose in discussing it was chiefly to throw into sharp relief the contrast between the historical and the cross-section viewpoints, and to make clear that my own theory was based on analysis of existing psychological forces. Since finding, however, that two writers for whose views I have so much respect have independently developed the same idea, and have taken it seriously, I have felt it worth while to give it this extended consideration.

Von Mises, like Wieser, needs an absolute value of money in his thinking. He does not call the concept by that name, but, following Menger[101] speaks of the "inner objective value of money" and the "outer objective value of money." (Mises, p. 132.) The latter is the purchasing power of money, a relative concept, exactly expressed in the price-level. The inner objective value of money is designed to cover the causes of changes in prices which originate on the money-side of the price relation alone.[102] This inner objective value of money performs the same logical function in the theory of money that the absolute social value concept of the present writer does, even though the psychological explanation lying behind it is very different.

Von Mises considers the quantity theory at length, noting a number of defects in it, chief of which is the fact that it has no psychological theory of value behind it, that it does not account for the *existence* of the value of money, and at most gives a law for *changes* in a value whose existence is taken for granted. The details of this criticism, however, need not be here presented. The quantity theory is to be treated in detail at a later point of our study.

The writer who has most definitely stated the relation of utility to the functions of money, is David Kinley (*Money*, ch. viii). He would explain the value of money, by (a) its utility as a commodity, and (b) its utility in the money-employment, the employments reaching a marginal equilibrium. The utility of the money metal in its commodity use calls for no analysis. But what is meant by the utility of money as money? Where the writers so far discussed have denied that money as money has any utility, Dean Kinley finds a utility in the money-function itself: money facilitates exchange, and exchange, by transferring goods from those who do not need them to those who do need them, increases the utility of those goods. Money, as money, thus produces utility.[103] The utility of money is the extra utility which comes into being by virtue of its use, as compared with what would exist in a state of barter. The marginal utility of money is the utility of money in the marginal exchange—the exchange which would be effected by means of barter if money were any more difficult to procure. The marginal utility of money, then, is not the whole of the marginal utility of the good for which it is exchanged, but rather is the differential part of that utility which is created by means of the use of money in exchange. The marginal utility of money, thus, appears in separate services of money. Money is a durable good, which gives forth its services bit by bit. The value of money is based on these separate services, it is "the capitalized value of the service rendered in the marginal exchange."

This conception is, it seems to me, much truer to the spirit of the general marginal utility theory than the theories of Wieser, Schumpeter, or von Mises. If the utility theory at large were valid, the application here would be valid. To Dean Kinley's conception of a marginal utility of the money service, I offer simply the objections which I offer to the utility theory at large—objections indicated in what has gone before, and in my *Social Value*. The application of the capitalization theory to the value of money I have already discussed in a previous chapter, and shall again consider in the chapter on "The Functions of Money."

I conclude that the marginal utility theory has not solved the problem of the value of money. The reason, however, is simply that it has not solved the general problem of value. The marginal utility theory, in so far as it seeks to make marginal utility the *cause* of value, is circular. The effect of a given man's wants upon the value of the goods he wants depends, not on the marginal intensity of those wants alone—a penniless prisoner may desire a marble palace ever so intensely without affecting its value—but also upon the value of the wealth possessed by the individual who experiences the wants. But this is to explain value, not by marginal utility alone, but by value as well—a circle. Or, if we leave the standpoint of absolute values, and look at the matter in terms of prices, the same situation presents itself. The price which an individual is willing to pay for a good depends on his income,—which commonly rests on prices—and on the prices he has to pay for other goods which enter into his budget. His price-offer, expressive of the marginal utility of a horse to him, is made with consideration of the price of a buggy, of harness, of feed, of the wages of the servant who cares for the horse, the price of a barn, and of the other things that the possession of the horse involves. And not these alone: less immediately, but still vitally, his whole budget enters. Higher prices for theatre tickets or for food or for clothing will reduce his price-offer for a horse. Further, his price-offer for the horse will be tremendously influenced by his opinion as to the permanent market price of horses. He will not be willing to pay a price for the horse which he cannot expect to get back if he should decide later to sell the horse. The direct influence of market price on individual demand-price is very great indeed. Marginal utility (subjective use-value) very frequently gives place to subjective value-in-exchange in the determination of an individual's marginal demand-price—which means that the market controls the individual instead of the individual controlling the market. With sellers, it is *generally* subjective-exchange-value, rather than marginal utility, that determines supply-price-offer. The sellers, in so far as they are producers, have little need for the great mass of their stocks. They will sell them, rather than keep them, at almost any price. The reason they ask high prices is simply that they think the market will give them the high prices. The individual price-offers, in the aggregate therefore, presuppose the whole market situation—presuppose a general value and price system already fixed and determined. Each individual price offer presupposes many other prices, though not, of course, the whole market. Since, then, much of the market situation is assumed in the determination of each particular price, by the Austrian method, it is obviously circular reasoning to think that the determination of each price separately by this method will supply data for a summary of the market situation as a whole. In the one form in which the utility theory avoids a circle,—that presented by Schumpeter, and discussed in an earlier part of this chapter—it is not a causal theory. Marginal utility is not a cause of market prices, but rather, marginal utilities and market prices are alike resultants, effects, of more fundamental factors. No writer[104] who has presented the utility theory in this form has tried to apply it to the value of money, and even if it could be so applied, it would not give a causal explanation of the value of money in terms of marginal utility. In most of the efforts to apply the utility theory to money, the circle becomes so obvious that one marvels that able theorists should for a moment fail to see it.

PART II. THE QUANTITY THEORY

CHAPTER VI

THE QUANTITY THEORY OF PRICES. INTRODUCTION

The quantity theory, in its usual formulations, is a theory, not of the value of money, in the absolute sense of value, but of the general price-level, the average price of goods exchanged for money. It is not a psychological theory. It does not deal with psychological quantities, or psychological forces. It is a mechanical theory, concerned simply with quantities, and the relations between them. The essence of the quantity theory comes out in the following brief statement: given a number of units of money; given a number of units of goods to be exchanged; assume these two numbers to be independent[105] of each other; assume all the goods to be exchanged for all the money; then the average price will be a simple function of the quantities of goods and of money respectively, such that an increase in the amount of money will increase the average price per unit of goods proportionately, if goods remain unchanged in amount, or an increase in goods will lower the price per unit proportionately, money being assumed to remain unchanged in amount. The qualification is commonly added that if goods have to be exchanged more than once, the effect is the same on prices as if there were an added number of goods equal to the added number of exchanges, and that if money is used more than once in exchanging a given number of goods, the effect is the same as if there were proportionately more money. Both quantity of goods and quantity of money are commonly defined as actual quantity multiplied by "rapidity of circulation." Rapidity of circulation, however, for both money and goods, is commonly thought of as a constant, so that the original formula remains unaffected by the qualification, so far as a prediction as to the effect of increase or decrease of money or goods on prices is concerned. Involved in the quantity theory, and explicitly stated by many writers, is the doctrine that the substance of which money is made is irrelevant, that it is the number, and not the quality or size of the money-units that counts. "In short, the quantity theory asserts that (provided velocity of circulation and volume of trade are unchanged) if we increase the *number* of dollars, whether by renaming coins, or by debasing coins, or by increasing coinage, or by any other means, prices will be increased in the same proportion. It is the number, and not the weight, that is essential. This fact needs great emphasis. It is a fact which differentiates money from all other goods and explains the peculiar manner in which its purchasing power is related to other goods. Sugar, for instance, has a specific desirability dependent on its quantity in pounds. Money has no such quality. The value of sugar depends on its *actual quantity*. If the quantity of sugar is changed from 1,000,000 pounds to 1,000,000 hundredweight, it does not follow that a hundredweight will have the value previously possessed by a pound. But if money in circulation is changed from 1,000,000 units of one weight to 1,000,000 units of another weight, the value of each unit will remain unchanged." (Irving Fisher, *Purchasing Power of Money*, pp. 31-32.) To the same effect is Nicholson's exposition, in which the money is assumed to consist of dodo-bones, the most useless substance that Nicholson could think of. For the quantity theory, prices are determined by the *numbers* of goods and dollars that are to be exchanged for one another, and not by the *values* of the goods and dollars;—indeed, for the quantity theory, "value" commonly has no meaning apart from the prices which are supposed to be adequately explained by the mechanical relations of numbers.

In the critical study which follows, virtually every doctrine and every assumption of this preliminary statement will be challenged. I shall deny, first, that the quantity of goods to be exchanged and the quantity of money to be exchanged for the goods, are independent quantities, maintaining, rather, that an increase in either of them tends normally to be accompanied by an increase in the other. Quantity of goods and quantity of money *exchanged* are not simple physical stocks, given data. Rather, they are consequences of human choices and human relationships, and vary from a large number of highly complex psychological causes, many of which are common to both. I shall deny, second, that "rapidity of circulation," either of goods or of money, is a simple constant, independent of quantity of goods or of quantity of money. I shall maintain, rather, that rapidity of circulation of money is a phenomenon which calls for psychological explanation: that the rapidity of money really means the *activities of men*; that these activities are complex, and obey no simple law; that instead of being an independent factor, constant, in the situation, the rapidity of circulation of money is bound up with the quantity of money, the quantity of goods to be exchanged, the rapidity of circulation of goods, and the prices of the goods, and that the rapidity of circulation of goods is likewise causally dependent on the factors named—or better, on the causes which control them; that rapidity of circulation, whether of money or of goods, is not a causal factor independent of prices, but rather in part depends on prices. In the third place, I deny the doctrine that the question as to *what* the money-unit is made of is irrelevant. On the contrary, I shall maintain that the *quality* of money, rather than its quantity, is the determining factor. I shall not maintain that only money made of or redeemable in valuable bullion can circulate, nor shall I maintain that the value of money depends wholly on the value of its bullion content when money is made of valuable metal. I recognize that value can come from other sources. But I shall maintain that value from some source other than the monetary employment is an essential precondition of the monetary employment, even though recognizing that that monetary employment may, in a way later to be analyzed, add to the original value of the money. The doctrine that only physical quantities, or abstract numbers, of goods are relevant I shall challenge especially, maintaining, on the contrary, that the psychological significances, the values, of goods are the really important thing, so that an increase in the number of one sort of goods may have a very different effect on the average of prices from an increase of the same number of units of some other good, and so that an increase in the number of goods exchanged under one set of conditions may have a very different effect on prices—or may be accompanied by a very different movement in prices, for the question of causal relations is a complicated one—from the change in prices that might accompany the same increase in the amount exchanged of same goods under other circumstances. Finally, the doctrine of the quantity theory that the price-level is a passive result of the other factors named: quantities of goods and money, and their respective velocities; that prices cannot initiate a change in the situation, will also be challenged. I shall undertake to show that the first change in the situation may appear in prices themselves, and that the quantities of goods exchanged, and of money, and their velocities, may then be altered to correspond with the change in prices.

I shall further maintain, as against the whole spirit of the quantity theory, that it does not seize hold of essentials in the causes lying behind prices. I shall contend that the factors with which it deals, instead of being independent *foci* to which converge the causes governing the price-level, and through which causation flows in one direction, are really not true "factors" at all, but rather are blanket names for highly complex and heterogeneous groups of facts concerning which few general statements are possible. Quantity of goods exchanged, for example, may be in some of its parts caused by rising prices, in others of its parts may be causing falling prices and is chiefly caused by *fluctuating* prices. The net change in prices in this case is not the result of any one movement from "quantity of goods" as a whole. Changes in the price-level are not one result, but rather, are the mathematician's average of many changes, due to a host of causes, in many individual prices. The quantity theory is an effort to simplify phenomena highly complex. Of course, the simplification of complex phenomena in thought is a laudable scientific goal, but when the simplification goes so far as to group things only superficially related, and to leave out the really vital elements, it is worthless. Value theory, with all the value left out, is like Hamlet with no actor for the title rôle. Simplification in the explanation of general prices has gone as far as we can legitimately take it when we seek to summarize all the factors involved in the *foci* of, on the one hand, the value of money, and, on the other hand, the values of the particular goods. The general price-level is an average of many concrete prices. Each of these individual prices has a concrete causal explanation. The *general* price-level has, not a few simple causes, but an infinite host of causes. Indeed, the general price-level has no real existence. It is a convenient mathematical concept, by means of which we may summarize the multitude of concrete facts. It is useful as a device for measuring changes in the value of money, on the assumption that changes in the values of goods neutralize one another. This assumption is never strictly true, and often is demonstrably false. The general price-level is neither a cause nor a result. Particular prices, in general, are results of two causes, namely, the value of money and the value of the good in question, and particular prices may then become causes, changing the quantity of money involved in a given set of exchanges. Neither quantity of money, nor quantity of goods exchanged, nor rapidity of circulation, nor general price-level is a simple, homogeneous quantity, obeying definite laws.

I shall also undertake to show that in many important cases the quantity theory leads to conclusions regarding the price-level which contradict other laws of prices, notably the capitalization theory, the cost of production doctrine, and the law of supply and demand. I have previously pointed out that these three doctrines are inapplicable to the problem of the value of money itself. On the assumption of a value of money, however,—using value in the absolute sense—they are applicable to the problem of prices, and, since the price-level is merely an average of particular prices, they should be applicable to the problem of the price-level also. It will be shown, in the course of the criticism which follows, first that the quantity theory contradicts each of these doctrines, in certain situations, and second, that in these cases, the conclusions based on the cost theory, the supply and demand theory, and the capitalization theory are right, and the conclusions based on the quantity theory are wrong. It has been maintained by certain writers, as Knut Wicksell[106] and Irving Fisher,[107] that cost of production and supply and demand are inapplicable to the problem of the general price-level. I shall maintain the contrary, holding that while these doctrines are inapplicable to the problem of the *value* of money, they *are* applicable to the problem of general prices, on the assumption of a fixed value of money. By the value of money I mean its absolute[108] value, and not—what the quantity theorists commonly mean—its "purchasing power," or the "reciprocal of the price-level."

I shall undertake to show that no sound conclusion reached on the basis of quantity theory reasoning is the peculiar property of the quantity theory school; that every valid conclusion which may be based on the quantity theory may also be deduced from the theory maintained in this book, and, indeed, that most of them may be deduced from several other theories of money, notably the commodity or bullionist theory. I shall show a number of false and misleading doctrines which logically spring from the quantity theory, and shall undertake to show that the quantity theory fails to give an adequate basis for several important parts of the theory of money, among them Gresham's Law, the theory of international gold movements, and the theory of elastic bank-notes and deposit-currency.

So much for the theses to be maintained. The detailed proof of these contentions will best be given in connection with a critical account of various versions of quantity theory doctrine. Attention will be given in this summary to the expositions of Nicholson, Mill, Taussig, and Kemmerer, and very special attention to I. Fisher, though some other writers will also be taken into account.

CHAPTER VII

DODO-BONES

Must money have value from some source outside its money-functions? It is a part of the quantity theory that this is unnecessary. I have cited, in the preceding chapter, Irving Fisher and J. S. Nicholson to this effect. Nicholson's statement is interesting and picturesque, exhibiting the quantity theory in all the nakedness of its poverty, and I shall present it at some length. "For simplicity," to isolate his phenomenon, he assumes a hypothetical market, in which the following conditions obtain: (1) No exchanges are to be made unless money (which he assumes to consist of counters of a certain size made of dodo-bones) actually passes from hand to hand. No credit or barter. (2) The money is to be regarded as of no use whatever except to effect exchanges, so that it will not be withheld for hoarding, *i. e.*, will be actually in circulation. (3) There are ten traders in the market, each with one kind of commodity and no money, and one trader with all the money (one hundred pieces), and no commodities. Further, let this moneyed man put an equal estimation on all the commodities. Now let the market be opened according to the rules laid down; then all the money will be offered against all the goods, and, every article being assumed of equal value, the price given for each article will be ten pieces, and the general level of prices will be ten. It is perfectly clear that, under these suppositions, if the amount of money had been one thousand pieces, the price-level would have been one hundred per article, etc. Under these very rigid assumptions, then, it is obvious that the value of money varies exactly and inversely with the amount put into circulation.—The rapidity of circulation he regards as coördinate, in fixing the price-level, with the volume of money. To illustrate this, he assumes again his hypothetical market, and "dodo-bones," assuming as before that one merchant has all the money (one hundred pieces), and that ten have commodities of equal value. Instead, however, of the merchant with the money desiring all the commodities equally, he is made to desire only the whole of that of trader one, who in turn desires the whole of number two's stock; and so on to the ninth merchant, who wants the commodity of number ten, *who wants the dodo-bones*. In this case, each article will be exchanged only once, as formerly, but the money will change hands ten times, and the price of each article will be one hundred instead of ten. "We now see that, under these circumstances, with the same quantity of money, and the same volume of transactions, the level of prices is ten times as great as before, and the reason is that every piece of money is used ten times instead of once." Whence he concludes: "The effect on prices must be the same when, in effecting transactions, one piece of money is used ten times as when ten pieces of money are used once."[109]

Ricardo, too, expresses the dodo-bone theory very explicitly. "If the state charges a seigniorage for coinage, the coined piece will generally exceed the value of the uncoined piece of metal by the whole seigniorage, because it will require a greater quantity of labour, or, which is the same thing, the value of the produce of a greater quantity of labour, to procure it.

"While the state alone coins, there can be no limit to this charge of seigniorage; for, by limiting the quantity of the coin, it can be raised to any conceivable value. It is on this principle that paper money circulates; the whole charge for paper money may be considered a seigniorage. Though it has no intrinsic value, yet, by limiting its quantity, its value is as great as an equal denomination of coin, or of bullion in that coin."[110]

Would the dodo-bones circulate? Nicholson chose the illustration to throw into the sharpest relief the absence of any value from a non-monetary employment. Nobody has any use for them as dodo-bones. What economic force is there, then, to make them circulate? Nicholson says nothing about an *agreement* among the traders, *assigning* a significance[111] to the dodo-bones, so that they might function in the same way that poker chips do—indeed, any such notion would vitiate his illustration, for he proposes to explain an adjustment of prices by natural economic laws. Why then, will any of the traders give up his valuable commodities for the worthless dodo-bones? Will you say that he will take them, not because he wants them himself, but because he knows that others will take them from him? But why would the others want them? Because they in turn can unload them on still others? But this seems a plain case of the vicious circle. It is, in effect, saying that the dodo-bones will circulate because they will circulate. A will take them because B will take them; B will take them because C will take them, C because ... N will take them; N takes them because A will take them.[112] I do not deny that if the traders used the dodo-bones as counters, agreeing that such dodo-bones should represent some other commodity chosen as a standard of values, that the dodo-bones would circulate. But, in that case, they would be, not primary, self-sustaining money, but merely representative, or token money. And just here let me lay down two general propositions[113] respecting the two main functions of money: to serve as a standard, or common measure, of values, the article chosen must, as such, be valuable. The thing measured must be either a fraction or a multiple of the unit of measurement. But this quantitative relation can exist only between *homogeneous* things. The standard, or measure, of values, then, must be like the commodities whose values it is to measure, at least to the extent of having *value*.[114] The second proposition is respecting the medium of exchange. The medium of exchange must also have value, or else be a representative of something which has value. There can be no exchange, in the economic sense—I abstract from disguised benevolences, accidents, and frauds—without a *quid pro quo*, without value balancing value, at least roughly, in the process. Now when it is remembered that the intervention of the medium of exchange, taking the place of barter, really breaks up a single exchange under the barter system into two or more independent exchanges, and that the medium of exchange is actually received in exchange for valuable commodities, it follows clearly that the medium of exchange must either have value itself, or else represent that which has value. These two propositions seem almost too obvious to require the statement, but they contradict the quantity theory, and they are not, on the surface, reconcilable with certain facts in the history of inconvertible paper money. It is necessary, therefore, to state them, and to examine further some of the phenomena which seem to contradict them. If they are true, Nicholson's dodo-bones will perform neither of the primary functions of money. They have no value, *per se*—they cannot, then, measure values; they are neither valuable nor titles to valuable things—they are not *quid pro quo* in exchange, and will not circulate.

I shall not pause long to discuss the doctrine that money needs no value itself, because it is really a sort of title to, or claim on, or representative of, goods in general. The notion, first, would not pass a lawyer's scrutiny. There are no such indefinite legal rights. A system of legally fixed prices, with a socialistic organization of society, would be necessary to give it definiteness—and in such a situation there would be no room for a quantity theory of prices! Economic goods, as distinct from money, are not generally "fungible" to the extent that would make them indifferent objects of legal rights. Besides, whether or not the thing is logically thinkable, it is legally false. Legal factors enter into the economic value of money, as will later be shown, but it is economic, and not legal, value, which makes money circulate. Helfferich has taken the trouble to give the notion of money as a mere title to things in general a somewhat more fundamental analysis, and I would refer the reader who is not satisfied by the foregoing on this point to his discussion.[115]

I wish to make very clear precisely how much I mean by the foregoing argument that circular reasoning is involved in saying that A will take the dodo-bones because B will take them. The same question arises for B, and for the others. The real question is as to the cause for any general practice of the sort. Why should A *suppose* that B will take them? What could bring about such a system of social relations that a general expectation of this sort could arise?

Kemmerer undertakes to give an answer in a hypothetical case by the following ingenious assumption (*Money and Credit Instruments,* p. 11): the money consists of an article which formerly had a high commodity value, which has lately entirely disappeared, but the money continues to circulate, through the influence of custom, and because of the demand for a medium of exchange.

In this illustration Kemmerer recognizes the historical fact that money has originated from some commodity which had value because of its significance as a commodity. Historically, a great many different commodities have served, and gold and silver finally emerged victors for reasons which need not just now concern us. These historical facts, coupled with the idea that value is, essentially, "something physical,"[116] or coupled with the notion that value arises only from marginal utility, or from labor, have been accepted by the Commodity or Metallist School as sufficient proof that standard money is only possible when made of some valuable commodity. Professor Laughlin seems to think of the whole thing as depending on the value of gold bullion, and to recognize the money-employment as a factor in affecting the value of money only in so far as it draws gold away from the arts, and so raises its value there by lessening the supply.[117] If money originated in a commodity, how is it possible for the commodity value to be withdrawn, and for money still to retain its value?

This brings us to a question I have raised before, namely, whether the genetic, or historical account of a social situation, and the cross-section analysis of the same situation, necessarily agree.[118] Is it possible that when a commodity basis was necessary to start the thing, and when even in the modern world gold bullion, interconvertible with gold coin, remains the ultimate basis of the money-systems of all great commercial peoples, that you could withdraw the commodity support and keep money unchanged in value? Or could you even have any value left at all? Now in answer, I propose to admit the possibility of so doing. The forces which a cross-section analysis reveals are not necessarily identical with those which a theory of origins sets forth. Once the thing is set going, the forces of inertia favor it. A new theory, fixed in the minds of the people, say the quantity theory itself, might give them such confidence in their money that its value might be maintained. A fiat of the government, making the money legal tender, supplemented by the loyalty of the people, might keep up its value. I think there is reason to believe that this is a source of no little importance of value for the German paper money to-day, and, to a less extent, of the notes of the *Banque de France*. All these possibilities I admit. Value is not physical, but psychological. And the form of value with which we are here concerned, economic value *par excellence,* is a phenomenon of social, rather than individual psychology. Many and complex are the psychical factors lying behind it. Belief, custom, law, patriotism, particularly a network of legal relationships growing out of contracts expressed in terms of the money in question, the policy of the state as to receiving the money for public dues, the influence of a set of customary or legally prescribed prices, which tie the value of money to a certain extent to the values of goods—factors of this character can add to the value of money, and can, conceivably, even sustain it when the original source of value is gone. Social economic value does not rest on marginal utility. In general, utility is essential, as one of many conditions, before value can exist, even though the intensity of the marginal want served by a good bears no definite relation to its value. But in the case of the value of a money of the sort here considered, marginal utility is in no sense a cause of the value. Rather, the marginal utility[119] of such money to an individual is wholly a reflection of its social value, and changes when that social value changes. It is quite consistent with the general theory of economic value which I have set forth in *Social Value,* for me to admit possibilities of this kind. The value of money in such a case has become divorced from its original presuppositions. The paper, originally resting on a commodity basis, or the coins originally valued because they could be transformed into non-monetary objects of value, have become objects of value in themselves. Analogous phenomena are common enough in the general field of values, and are less common in the field of economic values proper than one might suppose. Thus, most moral values tend to become independent of their presuppositions. Moral values of modes of conduct have commonly arisen because those modes of conduct were, or were supposed to be, advantageous in furthering other ends. Morality, in its essence, is *teleogical.* Yet so far have the moral ideals become ends in themselves that it is possible to have great thinkers, like Kant and Fichte, setting them up as eternal and unchangeable categorical imperatives, regardless of consequences. Thus Fichte declares, "I would not tell a lie to save the universe from destruction." Older still is the dictum, "*Fiat justitia, ruat coelum.*" Yet truth and justice, in the history of morals, and, in the view of most moral thinkers to-day, are of value primarily because they tend to preserve the universe from destruction, and would never have become morally valuable had they had the other tendency! Legal values manifest this tendency even more—one needs only to point to our vast body of technical rules of procedure in criminal cases, which persist long after their original function is gone, and after they have become highly pernicious from the standpoint of the ends originally aimed at. In the sphere of the individual psychology the phenomenon is very common. The miser's love for money is a classical example. The housewife who so exalts the cleanliness of her home that the home becomes an unhappy place in which to live, is an often-described type. The man who retires from business that he may enjoy the gains for the sake of which he entered business often finds that the business has become a thing of value in itself, and longs to be back in the harness, while many men, long after economic activity is no longer necessary, continue the struggle for its own sake. Activities arise to realize values. The value of the activity is derived from the value aimed at. But consciousness is economical, and memory is short. The activities become habits. The habits gather about themselves new psychological reactions. The interruption of habitual activities is distasteful. Life in all its phases tends to go on of its own momentum. The activities tend to become objects of value in themselves, whether or not their original *raison d'être* persist. In both the social and the individual sphere, apart from blind inertia and mechanical habit, active interests tend to perpetuate the old activities, whose *raison d'être* is gone. The judge who continues to apply the outgrown absurdities of adjective law may do it from timidity or from being too lazy to think out the new problems whose solution must precede readjustment to present social needs, but the criminal lawyer who can free his guilty client by means of these technicalities has an active interest in their perpetuation. The individual who would readjust his conduct in the light of changed interests finds that active opposition is met in the emotional accompaniment of the old habits. The economic society may wish to be free from a money whose original value is gone, but there is a powerful debtor interest which approves of that money, and whose support tends to maintain its value.

All these possibilities I admit. My own theory of value, which finds the roots of economic value ramifying through the total social psychological situation, rather than in utility or labor-pain alone, involves possibilities like these. But—and this is a point I wish especially to stress—we are out of the field of mechanics, and in the field of social psychology, when we undertake to explain the value of money that way. No longer is there any mathematical necessity about the matter. There is no such *a priori* simplicity as the quantity theory deals with. Factors like these might maintain the value of money for a time, and then wane. These factors might vary in intensity from day to day, with changing political or other events, leading the value of money to change from day to day, quite irrespective of changes in its quantity.[120] In so far as you have a people ignorant of the nature of money and of monetary problems, a people in the bonds of custom, with slightly developed commercial life, whose economic activities run in familiar grooves unreflectively, you will most nearly approximate a situation like that which Professor Kemmerer assumes. But that means that what might be true in India, or to a less degree in Austria—countries to which the quantity theorists are accustomed to refer—need not at all be true in the United States. Here everybody was talking about the theory of money in 1896—not necessarily very intelligently!—and here, moreover, such phrases as "good as gold," and propositions like that which came from Mr. J. P. Morgan in his testimony before the Pujo Committee that "gold is money, and nothing else," would seem to indicate that a very great part of our people might utterly distrust such a money as Professor Kemmerer describes. The banker's tendency to look behind for the security, to test things out, to seek to get to bed-rock in business affairs, holds with a great many people. An overemphasis on this is responsible for the doctrine of Scott[121] and Laughlin[122] that the sole source of the value of inconvertible paper money is the prospect of redemption, and that inconvertible paper money differs from gold in value by an amount which exactly equals the discount at the prevailing rate of interest, with allowance for risk, for the period during which people expect the paper money to remain unredeemed. We have not the banker's psychology to any such extent as that. Apart from the fact that the money function adds to the value of money, under certain circumstances,—a point to be elaborated shortly—other, non-rational factors, contagions of depression and enthusiasm, patriotic support, "gold market" manipulations, etc., entered to break the working of the credit theory of paper money as applied to the American Greenbacks. I may here express the opinion that the credit theory is the fundamental principle in the explanation of the value of the Greenbacks, however. But we have not the banker's psychology to any such extent as the extreme forms of that theory would assume. "Uncle Sam's money is good enough for me," is a phrase I have heard from the Populists,—who, by the way, were pretty good quantity theorists! "The government is behind it." There are plenty of men for whom that assurance would be enough. Indeed, the general notion that in some way, not specified, perhaps not yet known to anybody, the government will do what is necessary to maintain the value of its money is a ground which might well influence even the most sophisticated banker. I think such a general confidence in the English government has clearly been a factor in the price of Sterling exchange since the balance of trade turned so overwhelmingly against England in the present War.[123] Our monetary history, I may add, has been in considerable measure a struggle between these two opposing psychological reactions on that point. The utter breakdown of the *fiat* theory came in Rhode Island, and in connection with the Continental Currency, in the days before the Constitution was adopted. On the other hand, I do not believe that those who put a banker inside every one of us can prove that their principle has been a complete explanation at any stage of our monetary history. But clearly considerations like these take away all mathematical certainty from the matter.

The foregoing analysis makes clear, I trust, that the notion that the money function alone can make an otherwise valueless money circulate is untenable. There must be value from other sources as well. All that is conceded is that there need not be a physical commodity as the basis of the money. Value is not necessarily connected with a physical commodity.

There is a disposition on the part of many quantity theorists to beg the question at the outset, to assume money as circulating, without realizing how much this assumption involves. The assumption involves the further assumption that there are *causes* for the circulation of money. But the same causes which make money circulate will also be factors in the determination of the *terms* on which it circulates, *i. e.*, the prices. To seek then, by a new principle, the quantity theory, to explain these prices without reference to these causes, is a remarkable procedure. There is sometimes a disposition to do the thing quite simply indeed: define money as the circulating medium, and, *by definition*, you have it circulating! A rather striking case of this, which is either tautology or circular reasoning, appears in Fisher's *Purchasing Power of Money* (p. 129): "Take the case, for instance, of paper money. So long as it has the *distinctive characteristic of money,—general acceptability at its legal value,*—and is limited in quantity, its value will ordinarily be equal to that of its legal equivalent in gold." (Italics mine.)

It is not quite easy to construct, even ideally, a social psychology which would perfectly fit the quantity theory. One would have to assume that money circulates purely from habit, without any present *reason* at all. The assumption must be that the economic life runs in steady grooves, so that quantity of goods exchanged will always be the same, or at least, that it will always be the same proportion of the goods produced—there must be no option of speculative holding out of the market allowed the holder of exchangeable goods. The individuals must have constant habits as to the *proportions* of the money they receive to be spent and to be held for emergencies. All the factors affecting "velocity" of both money and goods must be constant—Professor Fisher maintains very explicitly that velocities, both of money and of bank-deposits are fixed by habit (*loc. cit.*, p. 152),—and, in any case, the assumption is necessary. A thoroughly mechanical situation must be assumed, where there is the rule of blind habit. Given such a mechanism, you pour in money at one end, and it grinds out prices at the other end, automatically. But, strangely enough, in this social situation where blind habit rules, prices are perfectly fluid! In India, or in other countries where the assumptions of the quantity theorist come most nearly to realization, so far as the general rule of habit is concerned, one finds also many customary prices. In a country completely under the rule of habit, the prices would, as a matter of *psychological* necessity, be also fixed. What might then be expected to happen in such a country, if an economic experimenter should disturb them in their habitual quantity of money? Which habits would give way, those relating to prices, or those to velocities, or those relating to quantities of goods exchanged?[124] I shall not trouble to solve this problem, as it seems to me not the most useful way to approach the problem of the value of money, but I submit it to the consideration of advocates of the quantity theory. My present purpose is accomplished in pointing out the psychological assumptions which the quantity theory makes: a psychology of blind habit, in a situation where the price-level is free from control by customary prices.

Now at another point I wish to mediate between the quantity theorists and their extreme opponents. Representatives of the Metallist of Commodity School—like Professor Laughlin, and Professor Scott in his earlier writings

—seem to deny that the money-employment has any direct effect in increasing the value of money. The money-employment affects the value of money only indirectly, by withdrawing the money metal from the arts, so raising the value of the money metal, and consequently raising the value of the coined metal. The quantity theory, on the other hand, would utterly divorce the value of money from causal dependence on the stuff of which the money is made. Both these views seem to me extreme. Unless money has value from some source other than the money employment, it cannot be used as money at all. Nobody will want it. On the other hand, the money use is a valuable use. Exchange is a productive process. Money, as a tool of exchange, enables men to create values. And you can measure the value of the money service very easily at a given time if you look at the short time "money-rates," *i. e.*, rates of discount on prime short term paper. These are properly to be considered, not interest on abstract capital, but the rent of a particular capital-good, namely, money. The money is hired for a specific service, namely, to enable a man to get a specific profit in a commercial transaction. Money is not the only good which can be thus employed, and which is paid for for this purpose. Ordinarily a man will pay for money for this purpose. Sometimes, however, one needs the temporary use of something else more than one needs money, and the holder of money pays a premium for the privilege of temporarily holding the other thing. I refer especially here to the practice of "borrowing and carrying" on the stock exchange. The "bear" sells stock which he does not possess, and must deliver the stock before he is ready to close his transaction by buying to "cover." He goes to a "bull" who has more stock than he can easily "carry," and who is glad to "lend" the stock in return for a "loan" of its equivalent in money. Ordinarily the bull is glad to pay a price for the money, as it is of service to him. Sometimes, however, the situation is reversed, and the service which the temporary loan of the stock performs for the hard-pressed bears is greater than the service which the money performs for the bulls, and the payment is reversed. When the bull pays a premium to the bear, for the use of the money, the amount paid is called "carrying charge," "interest charge for carrying," "contango," (London) or (in Germany) "*Report*." This is the usual case. But sometimes the bear pays the bull a premium for the use of the stock, and the charge is then called "premium for use," "backwardation," (London) or "*Deport*" (Germany).[125] Money is, thus, not the only thing which has a "use" in addition to the ordinary "uses" which are the primary source of its value.[126] In the case of other things, however, this kind of "use" is unusual. In the case of money it is the primary use. The essence of this use is to be found in the employment of a quantum of *value* in highly saleable form in facilitating commercial transactions. Commercial transactions, in this sense, are not limited to ordinary buying and selling. I think it best to defer further analysis of the money service to a later chapter, on the functions of money, which will best be preceded by a consideration of the origin of money. For the present, it is enough to note that money has certain characteristics which enable it to facilitate exchanges, and to pay debts, better than anything else, and that this fact makes an addition to its value. It is possible, I think, to measure this addition to value rather precisely in certain cases. Thus, in the case of the American Greenbacks, we find them at a discount, say from the beginning of 1877 on, as compared with the gold dollar in which they were to be redeemed in Jan. 1879. I think it safe to contend that the country was practically free from doubt as to their redemption after the early part of 1877. The discount steadily diminished as the time of redemption approached. Laughlin's theory is thus far beautifully vindicated. The central fact governing the value of the Greenbacks during this period was the prospect of redemption. But, and here I think we see the influence of the money-use, the discount was not as great as would have been called for by the prevailing rate of interest, as measured by the yield on other obligations of the Federal Government, at this time. And the discount completely disappeared some little time before the actual redemption. I see no cause for the absence of a discount in the later months of 1878 except the additional value which came from the money use. This additional value is, ordinarily, not very great. And money is not alone in possessing it. In extraordinary circumstances it may become quite large. Thus, in 1873, in the midst of the panic, the gold premium fell sharply. At this time the significance of the Greenbacks as a legal tender, a means of final payment of obligations (*Zahlungs-* or *Solutions-mittel*), as distinguished from medium of exchange (*Tauschmittel*), attained an unusual significance. In ordinary times, the marginal value of this function of money sinks to zero, but in emergencies it may become very great. In ordinary times, during the Greenback period, uncoined gold bullion, or gold coin used, not as money, but simply by weight in exchanges, played an important rôle, competing with the Greenbacks in various employments, particularly as bank reserves, and as secondary bank reserves, and so reducing the marginal value of the money-employment of the Greenbacks themselves. Gold bullion is not the only thing which can thus serve, however. To-day, and generally, securities with a wide market, capable of being turned quickly into cash, without loss, or capable of serving as the basis of collateral loans, up to a high percentage of their value, have a much higher value, for a given yield, than have other securities, equally safe, but less well-known and less easily saleable. The "one-house bond" (*i. e.*, the bond for which only one banking house offers a ready market) must yield a great deal more to sell at a given price than the bond of equal security which is listed on the exchanges, and has a wide market. Part of this is in illustration of another function of money, the "bearer of options" function, which enables the holder to preserve his wealth, and at the same time keep options for increasing its amount when bargains appear in the market. Foreign exchange performs many of these functions of money in European countries, particularly Austria-Hungary.[127]

The notion that the whole value of gold coin rests on its bullion content arises most easily in a situation where free coinage has long been practiced, and where there are no legal obstacles to the melting down of coin for other uses. Where free coinage is suspended, the peculiar services which only money can perform—or rather, the services which money has a differential advantage in performing—may easily lead to an agio for coined over uncoined metal. The mere fact that coined metal is of a definite fineness well known and attested is often of some consequence, though the attestation of well-known jewelers may give this advantage to metal bars as well, for large transactions. But for smaller transactions, nothing can easily take the place of money. A high premium on small coins, apart from redemption in standard money, may easily arise from the money-use alone. And standard coin may well attain, in greater or less degree, a premium. If it is scarce, as compared with the amount of business to be done, this premium may well be greater than if it is abundant. But that an indefinite premium is possible, or that this premium varies exactly and inversely with the quantity, I see no reason at all for supposing. If the premium be great enough, men, especially in large transactions, will make use of the uncoined metal—just as they did use gold in this country during the Greenback period. The advantages of money are not absolute. Money is simply more convenient for many purposes than other things. The possibility of a premium is limited by the possibility of substitutes. It is further limited by the fact that a high premium would awaken a distrust which would bring the premium to destruction, by destroying trade, and so destroying the money-use on which the premium is based.

A detailed discussion of the Indian Rupee since 1893 lies outside the scope of this chapter. I think it may be well, however, to recognize at this point that the limitation in the quantity of the rupee, through abrogation of free coinage, was a factor in the subsequent rise in its value. It was not the only factor, by any means. But it was a factor. It may be also recognized as a factor in the value of Austrian paper money.

The doctrine just laid down, as to the influence of the money-use in adding to the value of money, is in no sense the same as the quantity theory. For one thing, it is easily demonstrated that the value-curve for the uses of money is not described by the equation, $xy = c$. This curve expresses, in terms of value, the idea of proportionality which is an essential part of the quantity theory. Put in terms of the money market, we have a demand-curve for money, not for the long-time possession of money, but for its temporary use—a rental, rather than a capital value, is expressed in the price which this curve helps to determine. This curve is highly elastic. When money-rates are low, transactions will be undertaken which will not be undertaken when the rate is a little higher. In the second place, the method of approach is very different. It is not the whole volume of transactions which must employ money, but only a flexible part. In the third place, the money-use is here conceived of as a source, not of the whole value of money, but only of a differential portion of that value. In the fourth place, the argument runs in terms of the absolute value of money, and not in terms of the level of prices.

It is not the legal peculiarity of money, as legal tender, which is necessarily responsible for this agio when it appears. In the first place, not all money is legal tender. In the second place, we find the same phenomenon in connection with "bank-money" at times—I would refer especially to the premium on the *marc banko* of the Hamburg Girobank. (*Cf.* Knapp, *Staatliche Theorie des Geldes*, p. 136.) The legal tender peculiarity may, however, in special circumstances be a source of a very considerable temporary agio.

It is possible, however, to frame a hypothetical case in which, barring temporary emergencies, the money-use will add nothing to the value of money, and in which the whole value of money will come from the value of the commodity chosen as the standard of values. Assume that the standard of value is defined as a dollar, which is further defined as 23.22 grains of pure gold. Assume, however, that no gold is coined. Let the circulating money be made of paper. Let this paper be redeemable, not in gold, but in silver, at the market ratio, on the day of redemption, of silver to gold. This will mean that varying quantities of silver will be given by the redeeming agencies for paper, but always just that amount required to procure 23.22 grains of gold. Let us assume, further, that the government issues paper money freely on receipt of the same amount of silver. Assume, further, that the government bears the charges which the friction of such a system would entail, by opening numerous centres of issue and redemption, by providing insurance against fluctuations in the ratio of silver to gold for a reasonable time before issue and after redemption, meeting transportation charges, brokerage fees, etc. In such a case, the standard of value would not be used as money at all. It would have no greater value than it would if it were not the standard of value—abstracting from the fact that in the one case it might be used in its uncoined form as a substitute for money more freely than in the other. In any case, it would form no part of the quantity of money. Its whole value would come from its commodity significance. The value of the paper money, however, would be tied absolutely to the value of gold. As gold rose in value, the paper money would rise in value, and vice versa. The quantity of money would be absolutely irrelevant as affecting its value. The quantity of silver would be likewise irrelevant. The causation as between quantity of money and value of money would be exactly the reverse of that asserted by the quantity theory. A high value of money would mean lower prices. With lower prices, less money would be needed to carry on the business of the country. Paper would then be superabundant. But in that case, paper would rapidly be sent in for redemption, and the quantity of money would be reduced.[128] The value of money would control the quantity of money. The standard of value, which was not the medium of exchange, would control the value of money, and so the level of prices, in so far as the level of prices is controlled from the money side.

In this hypothetical illustration, we have the extreme case of what the Commodity or Metallist School seems to assert. In this case, barring temporary emergencies too acute to admit of increasing the money-supply by the method described, their theory that the value of money comes wholly from the commodity value of the standard, would offer a complete explanation. I offer this illustration as the antithesis of the dodo-bone illustration of Nicholson. That illustration sets forth the extreme claims of the quantity theory, and purports to be a case in which the quantity theory would work perfectly. The case illustrative of the commodity theory clearly brings out the fact that that theory rests on exclusive attention to the standard of value function of money. The dodo-bone theory gives exclusive attention to, but very imperfect analysis of, the medium of exchange function. But I submit that the extreme case of the commodity theory, in the illustration I have given, is a thinkable and consistent system. It would work—even though not conveniently. Indeed, it resembles in essentials the plan actually proposed by Aneurin Williams, and later by Professor Irving Fisher[129] for stabilizing the value of money. Substitute a composite commodity for gold, and gold for silver, in the illustration, and you have the essentials of that plan. The dodo-bone hypothesis, however, as I have been at elaborate pains to show in the foregoing, is unthinkable. It would not work. It is, thus, possible to construct a system for which the commodity theory would offer a complete explanation. It is not possible to do this for the quantity theory.

But the limiting case for the commodity theory is not the actual case. Standard money is also commonly a medium of exchange. Standard money is particularly desirable in bank and government reserves. Its employment in these and other ways is a valuable employment, and adds directly to its value both as money and in the arts. There is a marginal equilibrium between its values in the two employments. The notion that the only way in which the money employment adds to the value of money is an indirect one, by withdrawing gold from the arts, so lessening its supply and raising its value there, may be proved erroneous by this consideration: what, in that case, would determine the margin between the two employments? What force would there be to withdraw gold from the arts at all? Why should more rather than less be withdrawn? There must be ascending curves on both sides of the margin. Gold money in small amount has a high significance per unit in the money employment. A greater amount has a smaller significance per unit. The marginal amount of gold put to work as money has a comparatively low significance in that employment—a significance just great enough to secure it from the competing employments in the arts.

We conclude, then, that money must have value to start with, from some source other than the money function, and that there must always be some source of value apart from the money function, if money is to circulate, or to serve as money in other ways. But this is not to assert the doctrine of the commodity school, that its value must arise from the metal of which it is made, or in which it is expected to be redeemed. Nor is it to deny that the money function may add to the original value. On the contrary, the services which money performs are valuable services, and add directly, under conditions which we shall analyze more fully in a later chapter on the functions of money, to the value derived from non-pecuniary sources. Value is not physical, but psychical. And value is not bound up inseparably with labor-pain or marginal utility.

CHAPTER VIII

THE "EQUATION OF EXCHANGE"

In Professor Irving Fisher's *Purchasing Power of Money*[130] we have the most uncompromising and rigorous statement of the quantity theory to be found in modern economic literature. We have, too, a book which follows the logic of the quantity theory more consistently than any other work with which I am acquainted. The book deals with the theory more elaborately and with more detail than any other single volume, and sums up most of what other writers have had to say in defence of the quantity theory. Professor Fisher's book has, moreover, received such enthusiastic recognition from reviewers and others as to justify one in treating it as the "official" exposition of the quantity theory. Thus, Sir David Barbour cites Professor Fisher as the authority on whom he relies for such justification of the theory as may be needed,[131] while Professor A. C. Whitaker declares that he adopts "without qualification the whole body of general monetary theory" for which Professor Fisher stands.[132] Professor J. H. Hollander has recently referred to Professor Fisher's work on money and prices as a model of that combination of theory and inductive verification which constitutes real science.[133] The *American Economic Review* presents as an annual feature Professor Fisher's "Equation of Exchange."

Not all, by any means, of those who would call themselves quantity theorists would concur in Professor Fisher's version of the doctrine—Professor Taussig, notably, introduces so many qualifications, and admits so many exceptions, that his doctrine seems to the present writer like Professor Fisher's chiefly in name. But there is no other one book which could be chosen which would serve nearly as well for the "platform" of present-day quantity theorists as *The Purchasing Power of Money*. Partly for that reason, and partly because the book lends itself well to critical analysis, I shall follow the outline of the book in my further statement and criticism of the quantity theory, indicating Professor Fisher's views, and indicating the points at which other expositions of the quantity theory diverge from his, setting his views in contrast with those of other writers. We shall find that this method of discussion will furnish a convenient outline on which to present our final criticisms of the quantity theory, and parts of the constructive doctrine of the present book.

First, Professor Fisher presents in the baldest possible form the dodo-bone doctrine. The quality of money is irrelevant. The sole question of importance is as to its quantity—the number of money-units.[134] I shall not here discuss this point, as a previous chapter has given it extended analysis, except to repeat that it is in fact an essential part of the quantity theory. If the *quality* of money is a factor, a necessary factor, to consider, then obviously we have something which will disturb the mechanical certainty of the quantity theory. Professor Fisher is thoroughly consistent with the spirit of his general doctrine on this point.

Second, Professor Fisher has no absolute value in his scheme. By the value of money he means merely its purchasing power, and by its purchasing power he means nothing more than the fact that it does purchase: the purchasing power of money is defined as the reciprocal of the level of prices, "so that the study of the purchasing power of money is identical with the study of price levels." (*Loc. cit.*, p. 14.) In this, again, Professor Fisher is absolutely true to the spirit and logic of the quantity theory doctrine. The equilibration of numbers of goods, and numbers of dollars, in a mechanical scheme, gives prices—an average of prices, and nothing else. Any psychological values of goods or of dollars would upset the mechanism, and mess things up. They are properly left out, if one is to be happy with the quantity theory. Fisher, in discussion of Kemmerer's *Money and Credit Instruments*, has criticised the exposition of the utility theory of value with which Kemmerer prefaces his exposition of the quantity theory, as "fifth wheel." I agree thoroughly with Fisher's view in this, and would add that the only reason that it has made Kemmerer little trouble in the development of his quantity theory is that he has made virtually no use of it there! The two bodies of doctrine, in Kemmerer's exposition, are kept, on the whole, in separate chapters, well insulated. Coupled with this purely relative conception of the value of money, however, there is, in Fisher's scheme, an effort to get an absolute out of it: the general price-level is declared to be independent of, and causally prior to,[135] the particular prices of which it is an average. I mention this remarkable doctrine here, reserving its discussion for a later chapter.[136]

A further feature of Professor Fisher's system, to which especial attention must be given, is the large rôle played in it by the "equation of exchange." This device has been used by other writers before him, notably by Newcomb, Hadley, and Kemmerer, receiving at the hands of the last named an elaborate analysis. But Fisher, basing his work on Kemmerer's, has made even more extensive use of the "equation of exchange," and has given it a form which calls for special consideration.[137] The "equation of exchange," on the face of it, makes an exceedingly simple and obvious statement. Properly interpreted, it is a perfectly harmless—and, in the present writer's opinion, useless—statement. It gives rise to complications, however, as to the meaning of the algebraic terms employed, which we shall have to study with care. The starting point is a single exchange: a person buys 10 pounds of sugar at seven cents a pound. "This is an exchange transaction in which 10 pounds of sugar have been regarded as equal to 70 cents, and this fact may be expressed thus: 70 cents = 10 pounds of sugar multiplied by 7 cents a pound. Every other sale and purchase may be expressed similarly, and by adding them all together we get the equation of exchange *for a certain period in a given community.*"[138] The money employed in these transactions usually serves several times, and hence the money side of the equation is greater than the total amount of money in circulation. In the preliminary statement of the equation of exchange, foreign trade, and the use of anything but money in exchanges are ignored, but later formulations of the equations are made to allow for them. "The equation of exchange is simply the sum of the equations involved in all individual exchanges in a year.... And in the grand total of all exchanges for a year, the total money paid is equal in value to the total value of the goods bought. The equation thus has a money side and a goods side. The money side is the total money paid, and may be considered as the product of the quantity of money multiplied by its rapidity of circulation. The goods side is made up of the products of quantities of goods exchanged multiplied by their respective prices."

Letting M represent quantity of money, and V its velocity or rapidity of circulation, p, p', p'', etc., the average prices for the period of different kinds of goods, and Q, Q´, Q´´, etc., the quantities of different kinds of goods, we get the following equation:

$$MV = pQ + p'Q' + p''Q'' + \text{etc.}^{[139]}$$

"The right-hand side of this equation is the sum of terms of the form pQ—a price multiplied by the quantity bought."[140] The equation may then be written,

MV = Σ pQ (Sigma being the symbol of summation). The equation is further simplified[141] by rewriting the right-hand side as PT, where P is the weighted *average* of all the p's, and T is the *sum* of all the Q's. "P then represents in one magnitude the level of prices, and T represents in one magnitude the volume of trade."

It may seem like captious triviality to raise questions and objections thus early in the exposition of Professor Fisher's doctrine. And yet, serious questions are to be raised. First, in what sense is there an equality between the ten pounds of sugar and the seventy cents? Equality exists only between *homogeneous* things. In what sense are money and sugar homogeneous? From my own standpoint, the answer is easy: money and sugar are alike in that both are *valuable,* both possess the attribute of economic social value, an absolute quality and quantity. The degree in which each possesses this quality determines the exchange relation between them. And the degree in which each other good possesses this quality, taken in conjunction with the value of money, determines every other particular price. Finally, an average of these particular prices, each determined in this way, gives us the general price-level. The value of the money, on the one hand, and the values of the goods on the other hand, are both to be explained as complex social psychological forces. But when this method of approach is used, when prices are conceived of as the results of organic social psychological forces, there is no room for, or occasion for, a further explanation in terms of the mechanical equilibration of goods and money. Professor Fisher, as just shown, very carefully excludes this and all other psychological approaches to his problem of general prices, and has no place in his system for an absolute value. In what sense, then, are the sugar and the money equal? Professor Fisher says (p. 17), that the equation is an equation of values. But what does he mean by values in this connection? Perhaps a further question may show what he *must* mean, if his equation is to be intelligible. That question is regarding the meaning of T.

T, in Professor Fisher's equation, is defined as the sum of all the Q's. But how does one sum up *pounds* of *sugar, loaves* of *bread, tons* of *coal, yards* of *cloth*, etc.? I find at only one place in Professor Fisher's book an effort to answer that question, and there it is not clear that he means to give a general answer. He needs units of Q which shall be homogeneous when he undertakes to put concrete figures into his equation for the purpose of comparing index numbers and equations for successive years. "If we now add together these tons, pounds, bushels, etc., and call this grand total so many 'units' of commodity, we shall have a very arbitrary summation. It will make a difference, for instance, whether we measure coal by tons or hundred-weights. The system becomes less arbitrary if we use, as the unit for measuring any goods, not the unit in which it is commonly sold, but the amount which constitutes a 'dollar's worth' at some particular year called the base year" (p. 196). If this be merely a device for the purpose of handling index numbers, a convention to aid mensuration, we need not, perhaps, challenge it. The unit chosen is, in that case, after all a fixed physical quantity of goods, the amount bought with a dollar in a given year, and remains fixed as the prices vary in subsequent years. That it is more "philosophical" or less "arbitrary" than the more common units is not clear, but, if it be an answer, designed merely for the particular purpose, and not a general answer, it is aside from my purpose to criticise it here. If, however, this is Professor Fisher's *general* answer to the question of the method of summing up T, if it is to be employed in his equation when the question of *causation*, as distinguished from *mensuration*, is involved, then it represents a vicious circle. If T involves the price-level in its definition, then T cannot be used as a causal factor to explain the price-level. I shall not undertake to give an answer, where Professor Fisher himself fails to give one, as to his meaning. I simply point out that he himself recognizes that the summation of the Q's is arbitrary without a common unit, and that the only common unit suggested in his book, if applied generally, involves a vicious circle.

What, then, is T? Perhaps another question will aid us in answering this. What does it mean to *multiply* ten pounds of sugar by seven cents? What sort of product results? Is the answer seventy pounds of sugar, or seventy cents, or some new two-dimensional hybrid? One multiplies feet by feet to get *square* feet, and square feet by feet to get cubic feet. But in general, the multiplication of *concrete* quantities by *concrete* quantities is meaningless. [142] One of the generalizations of elementary arithmetic is that concrete quantities may usually be multiplied, not by other concrete quantities, but rather by *abstract* quantities, pure numbers. Then the product has meaning: it is a concrete quantity of the same denomination as the multiplicand. If the Q's, then, are to be multiplied by their respective p's, the Q's must be interpreted, not as bushels or pounds or yards of concrete goods, but merely as abstract numbers. And T must be, not a sum of concrete goods, but a sum of abstract numbers, and so itself an abstract number. Thus interpreted, T is equally increased by adding a hundred papers of pins,[143] a hundred diamonds, a hundred tons of copper, or a hundred newspapers. This is not Professor Fisher's rendering of T, but it is the only rendering which makes an intelligible equation.

We return, then, to the question with which we set out: in what sense is there an equality between the two sides of Professor Fisher's equation? The answer is as follows: on one side of the equation we have M, a quantity of money, multiplied by V, an abstract number; on the other side of the equation, we have P, a quantity of money, multiplied by T, an abstract number. The product, on each side, is a *sum of money*. These sums are equal. They are equal because they are *identical*. The equation asserts merely that what is *paid* is equal to what is *received*. This proposition may require algebraic formulation, but to the present writer it does not seem to require any formulation at all. The contrast between the "money side" and the "goods side" of the equation is a false one. There is no goods side. Both sides of the equation are money sides. I repeat that this is not Professor Fisher's interpretation of his equation. But it seems the only interpretation which is defensible.

A further point must be made: Sigma pQ, where the Q's are interpreted as abstract numbers, is a summary of concrete money payments, each of which has a causal explanation, and each of which has effected a concrete exchange. Mathematically, PT is equal to ΣpQ, just as 3 times 4 is equal to 2 times 6. But from the standpoint of the theory of causation, a vast difference is made. Three children four feet high equal in aggregate height two men six feet high. But the assertion of equality between the three children and the two men represents a high degree of abstraction, and need not be significant for any given purpose. Similarly, the restatement of ΣpQ as PT. One might restate ΣpQ as PT, defining P as the *sum* (instead of the average) of the p's, and T as the weighted average (instead of the sum) of the Q's. Such a substitution would be equally legitimate, mathematically, and the equation, MV = PT equally true. ΣpQ might be factorized in an indefinite number of ways. But it is important to note that in PT, as defined by Professor Fisher,[144] we are at three removes from the concrete exchanges in which actual concrete causation is focused: we have first taken, for each commodity, an average, for a period, say a year, of the concrete prices paid for a unit of that commodity, and multiplied that average by the abstract number of units of that commodity sold in that year; we have then summed up all these products into a giant aggregate, in which we have mingled hopelessly a mass of concrete causes which actually affected the particular prices; then, finally, we have factorized this giant composite into two numbers which have no concrete reality, namely, an average of the averages of the prices, and a sum of the abstract numbers of the sums of the goods of each kind sold in a given year—a sum which exists only as a pure number, and which, consequently, is unlikely to be a causal factor! It may turn out that there is reason for all this, but if a *causal* theory is the object for which the equation of exchange is designed, a strong presumption against its usefulness is raised. Both P and T are so highly abstract that it is improbable that any significant statements can be made of either of them. As concepts gain in generality and abstractness, they lose in content; as they gain in "extension" they lose (as a rule) in "intension." On the other side of the equation, we also look in vain for a truly concrete factor. V, the average velocity of money for the year, is highly abstract. It is a mathematical summary of a host of complex activities of men. Professor Fisher thinks that V obeys fairly simple laws, as we shall later see, but at least that point must be demonstrated. Even M is not concrete. At a given moment, the money in circulation is a concrete quantity, but the average for the year is abstract, and cannot claim to be a direct causal factor, with one uniform tendency. Of course Professor Fisher himself recognizes that his central problem is, not to state and justify, mathematically, his equation[145] —that is a work of supererogation, and the statistical chapters devoted to it seem to me to be largely wasted labor. Professor Fisher recognizes that his central problem is to establish *causal* relations among the factors in his equation of exchange. It is from the standpoint of its adaptability as a tool in a theory of causation that I have been considering it. It should be noted that "volume of trade," as frequently used, means not numbers of goods sold, but the money-price of all the goods exchanged, or PT. It is in this sense of "trade" that bank-clearings are supposed to be an index of volume of trade. The sundering of the p's and Q's really is a big assumption of many of the points at issue. Indeed, it is absolutely impossible to sunder PT. It is always the p aspect of the thing that is significant, Fisher himself finally interprets T, statistically, as billions of *dollars*.[146] As a matter of mathematical necessity, either P must be defined in terms of T or T defined in terms of P. The V's and M and M´ may be independently defined, and arbitrary numbers may be assigned for them limited only by the necessity that MV + M´V´ be a fixed sum.[147] But P and T cannot, with respect to each other, be thus independently defined. The highly artificial character of T has been pointed out by Professor E. B. Wilson, of the Massachusetts Institute of Technology, in his review of Fisher's *Purchasing Power of Money* in the *Bulletin of the American Mathematical Society*, April, 1914, pp. 377-381. "Various consequences are readily obtained from the equation of exchange, but the determination of the equation itself is not so easy as it might look to a careless thinker. The difficulties lie in the fact that P and T individually are quite indeterminate. An average price-level P means nothing till the rules for obtaining the average are specified, and independent rules for evaluating P and T may not satisfy [the equation.] For instance, suppose sugar is 5c. a pound, bacon 20c. a pound, coffee 35c. a pound. The average price is 20c. If a person buys 10 lbs. of sugar, 3 lbs. of bacon, and 1 lb. of coffee, the total trading is in 14 lbs. of goods. The total expenditure is $1.45; the product of the average price by the total trade is $2.80; the equation is very far from satisfied." Wilson thinks it necessary, to make the matter straight, to define T, arbitrarily as (MV + M´V´)/P in which case, the equation is true, but so obviously a truism that no one would see any point in stating it. T no longer has any independent standing. Fisher has, however, an escape from this status for T, but only by reducing P to the same position. He defines P as the *weighted* average of the p's (27), and fails, I think, to see how completely this ties it up with T. The only method of weighting the p's that will leave the equation straight is to weight the different prices by the number of units of each kind of good sold, namely, T. Thus, in Wilson's illustration, we would define P as [(5c.×10) + (20c.×3) + (35c.×1)]/14 P is then $10^{5}/_{14}$ c., while T is 14. PT is, then, equal to $1.45, which is the total expenditure, or MV + M´V´. Be it noted, here, that P is defined in terms of T, *i. e.*, P is defined as a fraction, the denominator of which is T. No other definition of P will serve, if T is to be defined independently.

But notice the corollary. P must be differently defined each year, for each new equation, as T changes in total magnitude, and as the elements in T are changed. The equation cannot be kept straight otherwise. Suppose that the prices remain unchanged in the next year, but that one more pound of coffee, and two less pounds of sugar are sold. P, as defined for the equation of the preceding year would no longer fit the equation. P, as previously defined, would be unaltered, since none of the prices in it had changed. P, defined as a weighted average with the weights of the first year, would, then, still be $10^{5}/_{14}$ cents. The T in the new equation is 13. The product of P and T is $\$1.34^{9}/_{14}$. But the total expenditure, (MV + M´V´) is $1.70. The equation is not fulfilled. To fulfill the equation, it is necessary to get a new set of weights for P, in terms of the new T of the new equation. From the standpoint of a *causal* theory, this is delightful. P is the *problem*. But you are not allowed to *define* the problem until you know what the *explanation* is! Then you define the problem as that which the explanation will explain!

Fisher, however, appears unaware of this. At all events, he does not mention it. And he ignores it in filling out his equation statistically, for he assigns one set of weights to the particular prices in his P throughout.[148]

The causal theory with which the equation of exchange is associated is as follows: P is passive. A change in the equation cannot be initiated by P. If P should change without a prior change in one of the other factors, forces would be set in operation which would force it back to its original magnitude. M and T are independent magnitudes. A change in one does not occasion a change in the other. An increase or decrease in M will not cause a change in V. Therefore, an increase in M must lead to a proportionate increase in P, and a decrease in M to a proportionate decrease in P, if the equation is to be kept straight. Changes in T have opposite proportional effects on P.

Before examining the validity of the causal theory, and the arguments by which it is supported, it will be best to state the more complex formula which Professor Fisher advances as expressing the facts of to-day. The original formula ignored credit, and ignored the possibility of resort to barter. It also failed to reckon with certain complications which Fisher deals with as "transitional" rather than "normal."

The formula which includes credit is as follows:

$$MV + M'V' = PT$$

Here, MV and PT have the same significance as before. M´ is the average amount of bank-deposits in the given region for the given period, and V´ is the velocity of circulation of those deposits. M, money, consists of all the media of exchange in circulation which are *generally* acceptable, as distinguished from those which are acceptable under particular conditions, as by endorsement. M excludes money in bank reserves and government vaults. Money, specifically, includes gold and silver coin, minor coins, government paper money, and bank-notes; M´ consists of deposits transferable by check. This version would not satisfy such a writer as Nicholson,[149] who would limit money to gold coin, and would include in M´ not only deposits, but also bank-notes, and other credit instruments. I may suggest here, what I shall later emphasize, that Fisher's "money," though he doubtless is using the most common definition of money, is really a pretty heterogeneous group of things, concerning which it is possible to make few general statements safely. In economic essence, *e. g.*, bank-notes are much more like deposits than like gold, and if one wishes to separate money and credit, bank-notes belong with M´ rather than with M. But we must take the theory as we find it! Again, credit is by no means exhausted when bank-deposits are named. Why should not book-credits, and bills of exchange be included? Why not postal money-orders, why not deposits subject to transfer by the giro-system? M´ is defined[150] as "the total deposits subject to transfer by check," and would, thus, exclude the giro-system of Germany. It is surely a very provincial equation of exchange, with which Fisher and Kemmerer seek to set forth the universal laws of money! Fisher's reason for excluding book-credits is that book-credits merely postpone, and do not dispense with, the use of money and checks.[151] Book-credits, unlike deposits, have no *direct* effect on prices (*Ibid.*, 82, n.; 370), but only an indirect effect, by increasing the velocity of money. (*Ibid.*, 81-82; 370-371.) Book-credit, indeed "time-credit" in general thus has no direct effect on prices, and is properly excluded from the equation of exchange. These distinctions seem to me highly artificial. In the first place, the use of checks, in part, merely postpones the use of money: money is moved back and forth from one part of the country to another, and from one bank to another, to the extent that checks fail to offset one another, and in the case of book-credit, while there is less of this offsetting, there is a good deal of it, especially between stockbrokers in different cities, and in small towns and at country stores, and particularly in the South, where the country storekeeper and "factor" are also dealers in cotton, etc., and where they advance provisions during the year to the small farmers, receiving their pay, in considerable degree, not in money, but in cotton, which they credit on the books in terms of money to the customer—a point which Fisher mentions in an appendix. (*Ibid.*, p. 371.) The difference on this point is a difference in degree merely.[152] Further, Fisher makes the same point with reference to deposits subject to check that he makes with reference to book-credits, namely, that their use increases the velocity of money. To say that one has a *direct* effect on prices, and the other only an indirect effect is absolutely arbitrary. If buying and selling are what count, if prices are forced up by the offer of money or credit for goods, and forced down as the amount of money and credit offered for goods is reduced, then one exchange must count for as much as any other of like magnitude in fixing prices. The same is true of transactions in which bills of exchange or other credit devices serve as media of exchange. Of course these considerations do not render the equation of exchange, as presented by Fisher, untrue. The equation simply states that the money and bank-deposits used in paying for goods in a given period are equal to the amount paid for those goods in a given period. It makes no assertion concerning payments for other goods, and makes no assertion as to the amount of other transactions which are paid for in other ways. General Walker, presented with the problem of credit phenomena, simplifies the thing even more.[153] He rules out all exchanges which are effected by credit devices, counting only those performed by coin, bank-notes and government paper money, and insists that the general price-level is determined in those exchanges in which money alone (as thus defined) is employed. His equation—if he had considered it worth while to use one—would then have been simply

$$MV = PT$$

where T would be merely the number of goods exchanged by means of money. One could make a similar equation, equally true, by defining money as gold coin, and reducing T correspondingly. Is there any reason for limiting the equation at all?[154] Is there any reason for supposing that any one set of exchanges is more significant for the determination of the price-level than any other set of exchanges? Does not the logic of the quantity theory require us to include all exchanges which run in terms of money?— If one wishes a complete picture of the exchanges, some such equation as this would be necessary:

$$MV + M'V' + BV'' + EV''' + OV'''' = PT,$$

where B represents book-credit, V'' the number of times a given average amount of book-credit is used in the period, E bills of exchange, and V''' their velocity of circulation, and O all other substitutes for money, with V'''' as their velocity of circulation. Even then we have not a complete picture, if direct barter or the equivalents of barter can be shown to be important.

For the present, I waive a discussion of the comparative importance of these different methods of conducting exchanges. The situation varies greatly with different countries. Fisher's and Kemmerer's equations are at best plausible when presented as describing American conditions, are much less plausible when applied to Canada and England, and are caricatures when applied to Germany and France.

So much for the statement of the equation of exchange, except that it is important to add that the period of time chosen for the equation is one year. Just why a year, rather than a month or two years or a decade should be chosen, may await full discussion till later. I shall venture here the opinion that the yearly period is not the period that should have been chosen from the standpoint of Fisher's causal theory, and that it probably was chosen, if for any conscious reason at all, because of the fact that statistical data which Fisher wished to put into it are commonly presented as annual averages. The question now is, however, as to the use to be made of the equation in the development of a causal theory.

CHAPTER IX

THE VOLUME OF MONEY AND THE VOLUME OF CREDIT

John Stuart Mill, who first among the great figures in economics gives a realistic analysis of modern credit phenomena, thought that credit acts on prices in the same way that money itself does[155] and that this reduces the significance of the quantity theory tendency greatly, and to an indeterminate degree. The quantity theory is largely whittled away in Mill's exposition of the influence of credit. In Fisher we have a much more rigorous doctrine. The quantity of money still governs the price-level, because M governs M´. The volume of bank-deposits depends on the volume of money, and bears a pretty definitely fixed ratio to it. Just how close the relation is, Professor Fisher does not say, but the greater part of his argument, especially in ch. 8,[156] rests on the assumption that the ratio is very constant and definite indeed. At all events, the importance of the theory, as an explanation of concrete price-levels, will vary with the closeness of this connection, and the invariability of this ratio. It is not too much to say *that the book falls with this proposition*, to wit, that M controls M´, and that there is a fixed ratio between them. We would expect, therefore, a very careful and full demonstration of the proposition, a care and fullness commensurate with its importance in the scheme. But the reader will search in vain for any proof, and will find only two propositions which purport to be proof. These are: (1) that bank reserves are kept in a more or less definite ratio to bank deposits; (2) that individuals, firms and corporations preserve more or less definite ratios between their cash transactions and their check transactions, and between their cash on hand and their deposit balances.[157]

If these be granted, what follows: the money in bank-*reserves* is no part of M! M is the money in circulation, being exchanged against goods, not the money lying in bank-vaults![158] The money in bank-vaults does not figure in the equation of exchange. As to the second part of the argument, if it be granted, it proves nothing. The money in the hands of individual and corporate depositors is by no means all of M. It is not necessarily the greatest part. The money in circulation is largely used in small retail trade, by those who have no bank-accounts. A good many of the smallest merchants in a city like New York have no bank-accounts, since banks require larger balances there than they can maintain. Enormous quantities of money are carried in this country by laborers, particularly foreign laborers. "The Chief of the Department of Mines of a Western State points out that when an Italian, Hungarian, Slav or Pole is injured, a large sum of money, ranging from fifty dollars to five hundred or one thousand, is almost always to be found on his person. A prominent Italian banker says that the average Italian workman saves two hundred dollars a year, and that there are enough Italian workmen in this country, without considering other nationalities, to account for three hundred million dollars of hoarded money."[159] I do not wish to attach too great importance to these figures, taken from a popular article in a popular periodical. It is proper to point out, too, that these figures relate to hoarded money, rather than to M, the money in circulation. But in part these figures represent, not money absolutely out of circulation, but rather, money with a sluggish circulation. And they are figures of the money in the hands of poor and ignorant elements of the population. Outside that portion of the population—larger in this country than in any other by far[160]—which keeps checking accounts, are a large body of people, the masses of the big cities, the bulk of rural laborers, especially negroes, the majority of tenant farmers, a large proportion of small farm owners, especially nominal owners, and not a few small merchants in the largest cities, who have no checking accounts at all. A very high percentage of their buying and selling is by means of money. Kinley's results[161] show that 70% of the wages in the United States are paid in cash, and, of course, the laborers who receive cash pay cash for what they buy. (Not necessarily at the *time* they buy!) Money for payrolls is one of the serious problems in times of financial panics.[162] To fix the proportion between money in the hands of bank depositors and non-depositors is not necessary for my purposes—*a priori* I should anticipate that there is no fixed proportion. But it is enough to point out that money in the hands of depositors is not the whole of Fisher's M. Of what relevance is it, then, to point out, even if it were true, that an unascertainable portion of M tends to keep a definite ratio to M′, when the thing to be proved is that the *whole* of M tends to keep a definite ratio to M′? Fisher's argument is a clear *non-sequitur*. If it proves anything, it proves that a sum of money,[163] not part of M, and another sum of money, an unknown fraction of M, each independently, for reasons peculiar to each sum, tends to keep a constant ratio to M´. This gives us *l'embarras des richesses* from the standpoint of a theory of causation! Two independent factors, bank-reserves and money in the hands of depositors, each tending to hold bank-deposits in a fixed ratio, and yet each moved by independent causes! By what happy coincidence will these two tendencies work together? Or what is the causal relation between them? And if, for some yet to be discovered reason, Professor Fisher should prove to be right, and there should be a fixed ratio between M as a whole and bank-deposits, would it not indeed be a miracle if all three "fixed ratios" kept together? Bank-deposits, indissolubly wedded to three independent variables[164] (independent, at least, so far as anything Professor Fisher has said would show, and independent in large degree, certainly, so far as any reason the present writer can discover), must find their treble life extremely perplexing. May it not be that Professor Fisher has pointed the way to the real fact, namely, that bank-deposits are subjected to a multitude of influences, no one of which is dominant, which prevent any fixed ratio between bank-deposits and any other one thing? At a later point, I shall maintain that this is, indeed, the case.

Be it noted further, however, that even if we grant a fixed ratio, on the basis of Fisher's argument, between M and M´, Fisher has offered no jot of proof that the causation runs from M to M´. He simply assumes that point outright. "Any change in M, the quantity of money in circulation, *requiring as it normally does a proportional change in M´*, the volume of deposits subject to check." (*Ibid.*, p. 52, Italics mine.) For this, no argument at all is offered. A fixed ratio, so far as causation is concerned, might mean any one of three things: (a) that M controls M´; (b) that M´ controls M; (c) that a common cause controls both. Fisher does not at all consider these alternative possibilities. I shall myself avoid a sweeping statement as to the causal relations among the factors in the equation, because I do not think that any of the factors is homogenous enough, as an aggregate, to be either cause or effect of anything. But if a generalization concerning these magnitudes were required, I should be disposed to assert that the third alternative is the most defensible, and that to the extent that M and M´ vary together it is under the influence of a common cause, namely, PT! That is to say, that the volume of bank-deposits and the volume of money tend to increase or decrease in a given market—and Fisher's theory is a theory of the market even of a single city[165]—*because of* increases or decreases in PT (considered as a unitary cause rather than as two separate factors) in that market. But I shall not put my proposition in quite that form, as I find the factors in the equation of exchange too indefinite for satisfactory causal theory.

So much for the validity of Fisher's argument, assuming the facts to be as he states them. Are the statements correct? Do banks tend to keep fixed ratios between deposits and reserves? Do individuals, firms, and corporations tend to keep fixed ratios between their cash on hand and their balances in bank? Regarding this last tendency, Professor Fisher says in a footnote on p. 50, "This fact is apparently overlooked by Laughlin." I think it has been generally overlooked. I have found no one who has discovered it except Professor Fisher. Certainly no depositor whom I have consulted can find it in his own practice—and I have put the question to "individuals, firms, and corporations." The further statement which Professor Fisher adduces in its support does not prove it, namely, that cash is used for small payments, and checks for large payments.[166] It would be necessary to go further and prove that large and small payments bear a constant ratio to one another, and further, that velocities of money and of bank-deposits employed in these ways bear a constant relation. If Fisher has any concrete data, of a statistical nature, to support the doctrine of a constant ratio between bank-balance and cash on hand in the case of individual depositors, he has failed to put them into his book. Nor is there any statistical evidence offered in the case of banks. It should be noted here that finding a general average for a whole country or community would not prove Fisher's point. General averages give no concrete causal relations. Fisher's argument, moreover, starts with individual banks and individual deposit-accounts (pp. 46 and 50) and generalizes the individual practice into a community practice. He would have to offer data as to individual cases.

While general averages could not *prove* the contention of a constant ratio between reserves and deposits for individual banks, general averages can *disprove* the contention. A constant general average would be consistent with wide variation in individual practices, on the principle of the "inertia of large numbers." But if the general average is *inconstant*, it is impossible that the individual factors making it up should be constant. This disproof is readily at hand, both for the ratio of deposits to reserves in the United States, and for the ratio of demand obligations to reserves among European banks (most of which do not make large use of the check and deposit system).

For the United States, from 1890 to 1911, taking yearly averages, we have a variation in the ratio of reserves to deposits of over 73% of the minimum ratio. The ratio was 26% in 1894, and 15% in 1906. "The juxtaposition of these extreme variations shows how inaccurate is the assumption that the deposit currency may be treated as a substantially constant multiple of the quantity of money in banks."[167] For New York City, the annual average percentage of reserves of Clearing House banks to net deposits varies from 24.89% in 1907 to 37.59% in 1894.[168] The extreme variations[169] in weekly averages are (for the sixteen years, 1885-1900) 20.6% in August, 1893 and 45.2% in February, 1894. These figures are extreme, since the number of occurrences is small for them, but there are numerous occurrences of deviations from the mean as wide apart as 24% and 42%.[170] The yearly fluctuation in all these ratios is very great.

The ratio of money held by the banks and money held by the people also shows wide variation, and considerable yearly fluctuation. There is a further complication, for the United States, of varying proportions of the total monetary stock held by the Federal Treasury. As between the banks and the public, the banks held about a third in 1893 (average for the year), and nearly half in 1911.[171] Whatever may be the relations between money in the hands of the people, money in banks, and volume of deposits, in "the static state," there is no statistical evidence whatever to justify the notion of fixed relations among them in real life.[172] We shall later show that there can be no static laws whatever governing the relations of credit and reserves.[173]

For European banks, the case is equally clear. European bankers deny any intention of keeping any definite reserve ratio. This appeared very clearly in the "Interviews" obtained for the Monetary Commission with leading European bankers.[174] The Banque de France increased its gold reserves, between 1899 and 1910, by 75%, but increased its discounts and advances during the same period by only 5%.[175] J. M. Keynes[176] points out that the reserves of the great banks of the world, and of Treasuries which act as central banks, have absorbed an enormous part of the gold produced in the fifteen years before the War, increasing their holdings from about five hundred million pounds sterling in 1900 to one billion pounds sterling at the outbreak of the War. "The object of these accumulations has been only dimly conceived by the owners of them. They have been piled up partly as the result of blind fashion, partly as the almost *automatic consequence,* in an era of abundant gold supply, of the particular currency arrangements which it has been orthodox to introduce.... The ratios of gold to liabilities vary very extremely from one country to another, without always being explicable by reference to the varying circumstances of those countries.... The contingencies, against which a gold reserve is held, are necessarily so vague that the problem of assessing the proper ratio must be, within wide limits, indeterminate. It is natural, therefore, that bankers, who must act one way or the other, should often fall back on mere usage or accept *that amount of gold as sufficient* which, *if they are chiefly passive, the tides of gold bring them.* [Italics mine.] At any rate, the management of gold reserves is not yet a science in most countries. There is no ideal virtue in the present level of these reserves. Countries have got on in the past with much less, and under force of circumstances could do so again."

It will be noticed that Keynes, in the passage cited, is speaking of *gold* reserves, while Fisher's contention relates to all kinds of money available for reserves, which in this country would include gold, silver dollars, greenbacks, and, for many State banks, the notes of national banks. He is also talking of the relation of reserves to demand *liabilities,* which for most great European banks are primarily notes, rather than of reserves to deposits. But as an exposition of the theory of the ratio of reserves to deposits (the chief liability of American banks), it is applicable to American conditions, and as a statement of the facts, it of course gives a basis for testing Fisher's doctrine generally. I do not think that Fisher's fixed ratio, as between reserves and deposits, or even the ratio which more moderate quantity theorists might seek to find between gold and demand liabilities, will find any justification in the facts of banking history.[177]

A factor which has developed on a grand scale in recent years has tended still further to weaken any tendency that may be supposed to exist toward a fixed ratio between money-reserves and demand-liabilities. I refer to the gold exchange-standard, in India, the Philippines, and elsewhere, and to the practice of the great banks of the continental countries of Europe, particularly the Bank of Austria-Hungary, of holding foreign gold bills, rather than gold exclusively, as reserve to cover note issue. In the case of the Austro-Hungarian Bank, which has carried this practice to the extreme, all possibility of a fixed ratio between gold reserves and demand-liabilities has vanished. The ratio is highly flexible. When bills are cheap, *i. e.*, when the exchange is "in favor" of Austria-Hungary, the Bank buys bills with gold; when bills are high, when the exchanges have turned "against" Austria-Hungary, the Bank sells bills for gold. Commonly, the holder of a note of the Austro-Hungarian Bank does not ask for it to be redeemed in gold, but in foreign exchange. The reason for this practice on the part of the Bank is primarily economy. A large holding of gold would represent idle capital—a heavy burden for the Bank of a debt-ridden and poorly developed country. Foreign bills, however, serve equally well for maintaining the value of the bank-notes, and at the same time bear interest.[178] A similar practice has been employed by the Reichsbank, by the National Bank of Belgium,[179] by virtually all the debtor countries of Europe, and the great trading countries of Asia.

Confidence in these conclusions is much increased by a study of the views of Professor Taussig.[180] Professor Taussig is, in his initial formulations of his doctrine, a quantity theorist. In a situation where only money is used, credit being excluded, in effecting exchanges, he would hold that the quantity theory correctly accounts for prices. He is fond of the old formulation, as a first approximation, even in dealing with the complex facts of modern banking. But he does not dodge the complex facts, and his theory becomes, substantially, first, a general formula, and second, an elaborate body of qualifications and exceptions, the latter making up the major part of the theory. His doctrine regarding the relation of money and credit is as follows: there is, in the long run, a real *limitation* on elastic credit instruments in the quantity of *specie*. (This is very different from the assertion that there is a *fixed* ratio between *deposits* and *money* in circulation, including paper, bank-notes, etc., in money. The present writer has no quarrel with the doctrine that the gold supply of the *world* imposes *outside* limitations on the *possible* expansion of credit.) The limitation, Taussig holds, comes in two ways: (1), in the connection between prices in any one country, and prices in the world at large; (2), in various links of connection between the volume of deposits (and of notes elastic like deposits) and the quantity of specie. I shall consider at a later point the relation between prices in different countries.[181] I shall there maintain that the quantity theory, which explains gold movements on the basis of price-*levels* in different countries, is inadequate; that not price-levels, but particular prices, of goods most available for international trade, are of primary importance, and that of these particular prices, one, namely the "price of money," or the short time money-rate, is most significant of all. For the present, I wish to analyze the linkages which Taussig finds between elastic credit instruments and specie, and to see how far they would go, not in proving Taussig's point (with which I have little quarrel) but in proving Fisher's contentions. The points involved are: (a) *Direct necessity* constrains the bankers to keep *some* cash on hand.[182] This fixes a *minimum limit* (Taussig's contention), but does not at all suggest a "normal ratio" (Fisher's contention). (b) *Binding custom*, as to the proper amount of reserve that banks should carry, particularly important in connection with the Bank of England, but also in evidence in the Banque de France and the Reichsbank. Here again, however, minimal, rather than fixed, ratios are suggested. Limitations on the *expansion* of credit these customs may impose, but they by no means determine a normal, or average amount of credit expansion— in England least of all, since there is so large a flexible element in the deposits of the Joint Stock Banks, whose reserves are largely secret. The statement *supra* quoted from Keynes, together with the testimony of European bankers, may be considered in connection with this point, also, as to the factors determining the reserve policies of the great European banks. The extent to which custom really binds is doubtful. (c) *Direct regulation by law*, peculiar to the United States. Here again, a minimum, rather than a fixed ratio, is indicated. Some *limitation* on credit expansion by the banks is caused by this at times, but Fisher's argument would require vastly more. (d) *The interaction in the use of deposits, notes, and other constituents in the circulating medium*. The point involved here is that different kinds of business call for different kind of media. Small retail business is not done with hundred dollar bills, nor are stocks and bonds bought with pennies. Limiting the size of bank-notes to five pounds in England compels the use of a large amount of gold for smaller transactions, and keeps a larger amount of gold in use than would otherwise be the case. Expanding business draws cash from the banks for circulation, trenching on reserves. That Professor Taussig has a point here is not to be doubted, but how closely it limits the expansion of credit will depend on the degree to which different kinds of media of exchange really *are* thus specialized. In a country like the United States, where checks may be used for virtually any transaction of over a dollar, and where small change for less than a dollar will be increased by the Government to meet the demands of trade, the point would not seem to involve a practically serious limitation.

Finally, Professor Taussig recognizes a coefficient with the quantity of specie in the *temper of the business community*. Whether or not deposits are to expand, depends not only on reserves, but also on the attitude of borrowers.

Taussig concludes: "Thus there is only a rough and uncertain correspondence of bank expansion with bank reserves; much play for ups and downs which have no close relation to the amount of cash in bank vaults, *and still less direct relation to the amount of money afloat in the community at large*. Where bank media, whether in the form of deposits or notes, are an important part of total purchasing power, the connection between general prices and quantity of 'money' is irregular and uncertain." (Italics mine.)

This conclusion would be of little service in supporting Fisher's rigorous contentions! Our constructive theory concerning the relations of reserves and deposits, or reserves and demand liabilities, must wait for later discussion, in the chapter on "Bank Assets and Bank Reserves" in Part III. It will there be maintained that there are no "normal" or "static" laws governing the percentage of reserves to demand liabilities, or to deposits, that the reserve function of money is a *dynamic* function, and that its whole explanation must be found in dynamic considerations. For the present, I am content to have analyzed two widely divergent views, one the extreme view of Professor Fisher, representing the quantity theory in its utmost rigor, and the other, the view of Professor Taussig, who virtually surrenders the quantity theory in complex modern conditions.

In between these two writers, verging more toward Fisher than toward Taussig, will be found, with great individual variation, the rest of the quantity theorists. The quantity theory, as an instrument of prediction, becomes important only to the extent that Fisher's view is maintained.

CHAPTER X

"NORMAL" VS. "TRANSITIONAL" TENDENCIES

The Quantity Theory, as a causal theory, is, then, little altered by the passage from a hypothetical, creditless economy to the actual world, where a vast deal of credit is used,—particularly in Professor Fisher's hands. Of the different kinds of credit, only deposits subject to check are recognized as directly influencing prices, and deposits subject to check are controlled by the volume of money. The causal theory[183] remains, then, as follows: if M be increased, it will increase M´ proportionately; it will not change the V's; it cannot increase T; to keep the equation straight, therefore, P must rise in proportion to the rise in M. A decrease of M, reducing M´ proportionately, leaving V's and T unchanged, must proportionately reduce P. P is passive. A change in P cannot sustain itself, unless it be due to a prior change in T, the V's, M or M´.

This theory is set forth with the qualification that these effects are the "normal" effects of the changes in question. The proportion between quantity of money and price-level is not strictly maintained during "transition periods." I now approach the most difficult question which I shall have to answer as to the meaning of Fisher's terms. The same problem arises for all quantity theorists. Precisely what is the distinction between "transition periods" and "normal periods"? What limitations and qualifications does he admit to the rigorous statement of his theory so far given? I may first express the opinion that the line shifts greatly in his own mind, or at least shifts greatly in the exposition. I do not find an explicit statement in which definitions are given. The matter is chiefly discussed by Fisher in ch. 4,[184] which is called "Disturbance of Equation and of

Purchasing Power during Transition Periods." There we find, as I have stated, no definitions, but the initial statements would suggest the following: a transition period is the period following a change in any one of the factors in the equation during which a readjustment among all the others is taking place; the normal period is the period preceding such a change, or following the transition after such a change, and is characterized by the fact that all the factors are at rest, in stable equilibrium. Equilibria during transition periods are unstable. During the transition, the relations among the factors vary: M and M´ need not keep their fixed ratio; P need not be wholly passive; M and P need not keep the same proportion. But until M and M´ get back into the normal ratio, until P becomes proportional to M (in the proportion prior to the initial disturbance), there is no rest; the equilibrium is unstable. How long is a transition period? How realistic is the notion of a transition period? Is the transition period a theoretical device, to aid in isolating causes, or is it supposed to be a real period in time? Is the normal period a real period in time, or is it merely a theoretical hypothesis? It is not easy to answer these questions. Thus (p. 72) the seasonal fluctuations are declared to be "normal and expected," and, at the same time, one gets the impression that Fisher considers them illustrations of his "transitions," in which the normal theory does not strictly hold (pp. 72, 169). What is described chiefly in the chapter on transition periods is the business cycle—a theory of the business cycle, based primarily on the notion that the failure of interest to rise as fast as prices rise causes the "boom," and that the draining of bank reserves precipitates the crisis. I shall not discuss this theory, as a theory of business cycles, further than to say that Wesley Mitchell's study would indicate that the interest rate is a minor factor, and that, while as a theoretical possibility, the drains on bank reserves may check prosperity if something else doesn't do it first, practically something else always does come in ahead, so far as his studies have gone.[185] My interest here is primarily in seeing the limitations Fisher imposes on his theory, and the qualifications he admits. If the business cycle is the typical transition period, during which his normal theory doesn't hold, when does the normal theory hold? When are the "normal periods"? There is no concrete period during which prices are neither rising nor falling, during which no important changes are taking place among the factors.[186] At times, Fisher seems to indicate that the normal period is imaginary (pp. 56, 159). Is, then, the contrast between a realistic "transition period" and a hypothetical "normal period" or are both hypothetical? Is the equation of exchange, too, a mere hypothesis? It should be, if it is to set forth a merely hypothetical theory. But no, Fisher insists on putting concrete data into it, and, indeed, gives an elaborate statistical "proof" of the equation. It, at least, is realistic. I confess that my certainty as to Fisher's meaning grows less, as I study his book with greater care. If the typical transition period be the business cycle, then the normal period could come only once, say, in ten years—or whatever period, regular, or irregular, one chooses to assign to the business cycle. The concrete price-levels for the greater part of the time are then surrendered to other causes. And the one-year cycle described in the equation of exchange is quite irrelevant. The equation of exchange should cover the whole business cycle, to fit in with the theory. Indeed, a realistic equation of exchange would then have no meaning at all, as the average price-level during the business cycle, played upon by a host of causes other than the factors described in the quantity theory, would not be the same as the average price-level which *would have* obtained had only the "normal" causes been in operation.[187]

The distinction between "normal" and "transition" *periods* suggests a dangerous fallacy: namely, that during one period one sort of causation is working, with the other in abeyance. In fact, whatever causes there are are working all the time. The only legitimate thing is to abstract from one set of causes, and see what the other set, if left to themselves, will bring about. But this sort of abstraction has many dangers, one of which is that the causes abstracted from are frequently thought of as non-existent. The chemist, in his laboratory, can in actual physical fact abstract impurities from his chemicals, and see what they will do. He can even perform experiments in what is practically a vacuum. But the economist has no right to *think in vacuo*! All that he has a right to do is to assume the factors which he does not wish to study *constant*. And even that he must not do if (1) changes in the factors which he wishes to study do in fact lead to changes in the factors abstracted from, or (2) if the factors which he wishes to study can only change *because* of prior or concomitant changes in the factors from which he is abstracting. Is it, for example, legitimate to assume an increase in M´ apart from its usual accompaniment, an increase in PT?

The notion, too, that causation can be seen in a state of stable equilibrium should be critically analyzed. Causation is only *revealed* by a *course of events*, when mechanical causation is involved. The relation of cause and effect may be a contemporaneous relation in fact, and it is possible, where conscious, psychological phenomena are involved, to discern causal relations among the elements in a mental state by direct introspection. It is the not uncommon practice, also, in the theory of mechanics, or in theoretical economics, where the method of investigation is deductive rather than inductive, to abstract from the temporal sequence, and to construe causal relations as timeless, logical relations. But even here, the cause of a *change* in the general situation precedes the change in time, and it is only by abstraction that the time element is left out. If there is no question as to the causal relations, this abstraction is legitimate, but if all that one knows about the situation be that in a stable equilibrium certain constant ratios obtain, then the question as to which term in the ratio is cause and which is effect remains unanswered. In Fisher's situation, then, assuming that it be true—which I shall deny—that the only stable equilibrium is that which the normal theory requires, it still remains true that the causal relations among the factors can only be revealed by a study of the transitions, by seeing the temporal sequence of changes in the factors of the equation. Even if it be granted that M, M´ and P tend to keep a constant relation to one another, the quantity theory falls if, for instance, it can be shown that a change may first occur in P, spread to M´, and finally reach M last of all, leading to a new normal equilibrium which is stable. I shall later show cases of this sort.[188]

The abstract formulation of Fisher's contrast will not, I believe, give us an answer as to the extent to which he thinks his quantity theory realistic. I find myself particularly in genuine uncertainty as to the point mentioned above: would an actual equation of exchange for the whole business cycle, made up of the averages of M, M´, V, V´, P and T for the whole period, exhibit the "normal" relations among these factors? Or would this "normal" relation only emerge concretely at some moment of time in the course of the cycle when the abnormal causes affecting the price-level happened to offset one another? Or is it true that no actual figures which might be found, either for a moment of time, or as averages for any given period, will exhibit the relations required, and that only a hypothetical equation, based on the figures for M, M´, V, V´, P and T that *would have been realized* had there been no "disturbing" causes, will show these "normal" relations? If, as

Fisher at times indicates—as in his reference to Boyle's Law (p. 296)—he is stating only an abstract tendency, which may be neutralized by other tendencies in the situation, so far as concrete results are concerned, then it is this last doctrine which we must take, and the concrete equation of exchange has little if any relevance. If, moreover, this last interpretation be given, then the whole of Fisher's elaborate statistical "proof" is pointless. The only sort of statistical proof which would be relevant would be of a much subtler sort, not a mere filling out of the equation of exchange by means of annual figures, but an effort to disentangle and measure the *importance* of his tendency, as compared with other tendencies. But we have the other tendencies merely mentioned in qualitative terms, and we never find any definite statement, of mathematical character, as to how important they are.

It seems pretty clear, however, that on the whole, despite occasional suggestions that his theory is abstract, Fisher means his theory to be the overwhelmingly important point in the explanation of actual price-levels. He is particularly insistent on the high degree of the generality of his contention that P is passive. Thus: "So far as I can discover, *except to a* LIMITED *extent during transition periods, or during a passing season,* (*e. g., the fall*) (capitals mine, italics Fisher's), there is no truth whatever in the idea that the price-level is an independent cause of changes in any of the other magnitudes, M, M´, V, V´, or the Q's."[189] On p. 182 he enumerates in a series of propositions his general normal theory, and adds, as the first sentence of proposition 9: "Some of the foregoing propositions *are subject to* SLIGHT *modification during transition periods*." (Italics and capitals mine.) And the general drift of the argument, particularly in chapter 8, where the heart of Fisher's causal theory is presented, would indicate that the concessions he is disposed to make are very slight, indeed.

The question as to how long a *time* is required, in Fisher's view, for a transition to occur, and for his normal tendencies to dominate, is nowhere made clear. The quantity theory, in the hands of some writers, is a very long run theory, for others, it is a short run theory. Thus, Taussig would make the "run" exceedingly long.[190] Mill makes it a short run theory. "It is not, however, with ultimate or average, but with immediate and temporary prices, that we are now concerned. These, as we have seen, may deviate widely from the standard of cost of production. Among other causes of fluctuation, one we have found to be, the quantity of money in circulation. Other things being the same, an increase of the money in circulation raises prices, a diminution lowers them. If more money is thrown into circulation than the quantity which can circulate at a value conformable to its cost of production, the value of money, so long as the excess lasts, will remain below the standard of cost of production, and general prices will be sustained above the natural rate."[191] I pause to note that it is really strange that a single name should describe theories so different, resting on such essentially different logic. Long run or short run theories, all are "quantity theories," whether "money" be defined as gold, or as all manner of media of exchange, or as only those media of exchange which pass from hand to hand without endorsement. Fisher would doubtless call his theory a long run theory. From the standpoint of the notion that "prices ... lag behind their full adjustment and have to be pushed up, so to speak, by increased purchases,"[192] however, we get a short run quantity theory doctrine. The logic of these two is very different. The short run doctrine seeks to explain the actual process of price-making in the market. Money is offered against goods, and the actual quantities on each side determine the momentary price-level, concretely. Or, when credit is considered, money and credit offered against goods, at a given time, or in a given short period, determine the actual price-level reached. This is the logic of the equation of exchange—actual money paid is necessarily equal to actual money received. The long run doctrine is fundamentally based on a different notion. Surrendering the actual or average of price-levels to other causes, in part, it still asserts that, given time enough, and barring new disturbing tendencies, a price-level will ultimately be reached which will bear it out. I find no recognition, on Fisher's part, of the fact that these two doctrines are different, and, in fact, I find them blended and confused in the course of his argument. He would doubtless maintain that his is a long run doctrine. But how long is the "run"? Sometimes it seems to be, as already shown, a whole business cycle. Sometimes a passing season, as the fall. When he undertakes to apply his theory to a practical proposal for regulating the value of money, he relies on the quantity theory tendency to bring about adjustments so quickly that it is worth while to make *monthly* adjustments in anticipation of it.[193] When discussing the changes in gold premium on the Greenbacks during the exciting times of the Civil War, he relies so thoroughly on his theory that he will not allow even the rapid change of four per cent in a single day following Chickamauga to occur except in conformity with the quantity theory. This last statement is so remarkable that I must quote Fisher himself: "It would be a grave mistake to reason, because the losses at Chickamauga caused greenbacks to fall 4% in a single day, that their value had no relation to their volume. This fall indicated a slight acceleration in the velocity of circulation, and a slight retardation in the volume of trade" (263). It would be indeed remarkable if the changes in the gold market, which got war news before the newspapers got it, and where changes in gold premium occurred before the rest of the country could possibly react to the war news, should be controlled by V and T! I had not supposed that the most rigorous of short run quantity theorists would make any such demands on his theory as that. Indeed, I had not supposed that the quantity theory would feel called on to explain the gold premium, as such, except in so far as the gold premium is an index of general prices.

Finding it impossible to limit Fisher to any single statement of the quantitative importance of his normal theory as compared with the other tendencies at work, but concluding that, on the whole, he considers it of high importance, I shall now proceed to an analysis of the reasoning by which he seeks to justify it as a *qualitative* tendency. I shall maintain that, however long or short the period required, however strong or weak the tendency he defends, the reasoning by which he seeks to justify it is unsound, and that even as a qualitative tendency, the quantity theory is invalid. At a later part of the book, as in an earlier part,[194] I shall undertake to find the modicum of truth which the quantity theory contains, and shall show that no quantity theory is needed to exhibit this modicum of truth.

CHAPTER XI

BARTER

In the statement of the quantity theory, the proviso is commonly made that all exchanges must be made by means of money, or of money and bank-credit. Barter is excluded by hypothesis. If resort to barter were possible, then people might avert the fall in prices due to scarcity of money, or increase in trade, by dispensing with money in part of their transactions, and the proportional decrease in prices which the quantity theory calls for would be lacking. Is this assumption true? Is barter banished from the modern world, or does it remain reasonably possible, and, to a considerable degree, actual?

Fisher maintains the thesis—the failure of which he admits would spoil the quantity theory[195]—that barter is practically impossible, and negligible in modern business life. "Practically, however, in the world to-day, even such temporary resort to barter is trifling. The convenience of exchange by money is so much greater than the convenience of barter, that the price adjustment would be made almost at once. If barter needs to be seriously considered as a relief from money stringency, we shall be doing it full justice if we picture it as a safety valve, working against a resistance so great as almost never to come into operation, and then only for brief transition intervals. For all practical purposes and all normal cases, we may assume that money and checks are necessities for modern trade."[196]

This contention seems to me untenable. I think it can easily be shown that barter remains an important factor in modern business life, especially if one extends the term barter, a little, to cover various flexible substitutes for the use of money and checks in effecting exchanges. Clearly from the standpoint of the present issue, such an extension of the meaning of barter is legitimate, as any such substitutes would equally spoil the proportionality in the supposed relation between prices and money, or prices and trade.

Where does one find barter? Well, not to be ignored would be the advertisements which fill many columns of such a paper as the New York *Telegram* in the course of a week; "Wanted: to trade a well-trained parrot for a violin"—a trade that might, or might not, be a wise one! There is a good deal of such simple barter among the people. Then, perhaps more important, is the regular practice of sewing machine, piano, automobile, and other similar companies of taking part of the payment for a new machine, piano,[197] or automobile in the similar thing which the owner is discarding. The old machine, piano, etc., are then repaired, repainted, and sold again. This is a very extensive practice. Again, there are companies which combine the business of wrecking old houses and building new ones, who regularly take the old materials as part of their pay. This is a highly important feature of the organized building trade in great cities, and is frequently done in small towns. The building trade is no negligible matter. The "horse-trade" still thrives in rural regions, and barter of various kinds, of live stock, of grain and hay, of fresh and cured meat, and of labor, is an important feature in rural life in many sections. Much of agricultural rent in the South is still paid in kind, under the "share system." Much labor, especially farm and domestic labor, is still paid for partly in kind. Where payments for labor are made in orders on company stores, we have again what is virtually barter, from the standpoint of the point at issue. *Real estate* transactions make large use of barter. Farms are exchanged for one another, with some cash (or more usually, a promissory note) "to boot." The writer has repeatedly heard real estate men say to customers: "I can't sell it for you very easily, but I can trade it off, and maybe you can sell what you trade it for." This is perhaps more frequent in rural real estate transactions, and in the smaller cities, than in large cities, but it is very extensive in New York City.[198]

Again, when corporations are to be combined, various plans are possible. There may be a merger; there may be a holding corporation; there may be a lease. If the money market is easy, one of the former methods will be used, —most frequently, for legal reasons, the holding corporation, if there are any valuable franchises involved. But mergers and holding corporations commonly involve buying out the interests which are to be absorbed, and call for the use of checks. If the money market is tight, therefore, the promoter of the combination may frequently find the lease the more advantageous form of consolidation.[199] The great advantage of the lease is that, when the money market is tight, it involves no *financial plan*, no underwriting, no outlay of "cash." This is, therefore, an equivalent of barter, so far as the point at issue is concerned. Even where a holding corporation is formed, however, there may be considerable barter: the stockholders of the corporation which is absorbed may receive payment for their stocks, in whole or in part, in the securities of the holding company, rather than in checks. An era of financial consolidation, such as we have been passing through, and through which we have not by any means gone, though the movement toward *monopoly* has been in great degree checked, presents a great deal of this sort of barter, or equivalents of barter.[200] A striking thing to notice here, moreover, is the flexible margin between use of bank-credit and barter, a margin depending primarily upon the condition of the money market, and particularly upon the money-rates.

Not yet has the most important element in modern barter been mentioned. I refer to the "clearing-house" arrangements of the stock and produce exchanges. Under these arrangements, brokers who have sold ten thousand shares of Westinghouse El. and M. Common during the day, and bought seven thousand shares, buying and selling being in smaller lots, with a number of different houses, no longer are obliged to deliver ten thousand shares, receiving therefor $700,000, and to receive seven thousand shares, paying therefor $490,000. Instead, they deliver three thousand shares only to the clearing house, and receive from the clearing house only $210,000 when the transaction is, from the standpoint of the particular broker involved, completed. This is a far remove, in technical perfection, from primitive barter, but it is barter, and it saves the using of a vast deal of bank-credit as between brokers. How important it is, from the standpoint of the stock exchange, may be judged from the following statement in Sprague's *Crises Under the National Banking System*: "A much more fundamental change in the organization in the New York money market came with the establishment of the stock exchange clearing house in May, 1892. It led to a very considerable reduction in the *clearing-house exchanges of the banks* and also, and more important, in the volume of certified checks. [Italics mine.] Overcertification of checks ceased to be a factor of the first magnitude in the banking methods of the city. Had not this arrangement for stock-exchange dealings been set up, it is probable that it would have been necessary to close the stock exchange in 1893 and in 1907, and it is also probable that the volume of business transacted in the years after 1897 could not have been handled." (P. 152.)

The same arrangements have been widely introduced in other stock exchanges, and in the produce exchanges.[201]

In general, with reference to barter, this point is significant. The money economy has made barter *easier* rather than harder. It has made possible a host of refinements in barter, which make it at many points more convenient and cheaper than check or money exchanges. It is common to find our present methods of conducting foreign trade described as a "system of refined barter," which indeed, from the standpoint of the present issue, it is: bills of exchange are neither money nor bank-credit! Where bills of exchange are used in internal trade extensively—as in Germany, where they pass from hand to hand in several transactions before being discounted at banks[202]—we have a highly important substitute for money and deposits, which functions as barter,—flexibility of substitutes for money and deposits is strikingly evident. The feature of the money economy which has thus refined and improved barter is the *standard of value (common measure of value)* function of money.[203] This standard of value function, be it noted, makes no call on money itself, necessarily. The *medium of exchange* and "*bearer of options*" functions of money are the chief sources of such additions to the value of money as come from the money-use. But the fact that goods have money-prices, which can be compared with one another easily, in objective terms, makes barter, and barter-equivalents, a highly convenient and very important feature of the most developed commercial system. And so we reject another essential assumption of the quantity theory.[204]

CHAPTER XII

VELOCITY OF CIRCULATION

For the quantity theory, it is important to treat velocity of circulation of money and of deposits, as self-contained entities, really independent factors. This is true of Fisher's theory. It is particularly necessary that V and V´ should vary from causes unconnected with M and M´. The V's are to be a sort of inflexible channel, through which M and M´ run in their influence on the passive P, which is to rise or fall proportionately with them. If an increase of M or M´ should lead to a reduction in the V's, if people, having more money available, should be less assiduous in using every bit of it in effecting exchanges, then P would not rise in proportion to the increase in M. Complete demonstration of Fisher's thesis, therefore, requires the proof of the negative proposition that V does not change as a consequence of changes in M or M´. This proof Fisher finds in the contention that the V's are fixed by the habits and conveniences of individuals, whence they are not influenced by such a cause as a change in the amount of money.[205]

V is defined,[206] not as the number of times a given dollar is exchanged in a given year (the "coin-transfer" notion), but as a social average based on the average number of coins which pass through *each man's* hands, divided by the average amount held by him (the "person-turnover" concept of velocity.) V´ is similarly defined. Fisher asserts that both concepts, if correctly employed, lead to the same result. I would point out one important difference between them here: if money is *short-circuited*, if, *i. e.*, a part of the economic community loses its incomes, or finds its incomes reduced, then the "velocity of money," on the "coin-transfer" basis is reduced, provided the "person-turnover" average remains the same, while on the "person-turnover" basis the velocity will remain unchanged. It is clearly the "coin-transfer" concept which is fundamental, from the standpoint of the equation of exchange, and Fisher feels justified in using the other method only because he considers it an equivalent of the "coin-transfer" concept. I shall later show cases where the distinction between the two concepts is all-important, particularly in the case where T is reduced by the elimination of *middlemen*.[207]

The conception of velocity of circulation as a real, unitary entity, a *cause*, in the process of price-determination, is, I suppose, almost as old as the quantity theory itself. It is an essential part of the quantity theory. To me "velocity of circulation" seems to be a mere name, denoting, not any simple cause or small set of causes, which can exert a specific influence, but rather a meaningless abstract number, which is the non-essential by-product of a highly heterogeneous lot of *activities of men*, some of which work one way, and others of which work in another way, in affecting prices. It is at best a passive *resultant* of conflicting and divergent tendencies, and has, to my mind, no more *causal* significance than the average of the abstract numbers of yards gained by both sides, heights and weights of players, kick-offs, and minutes taken out for injuries, would have on the result of the Yale-Harvard game. The real causes of changes in prices lie deeper! I should expect V and V′ to be the most highly flexible factors in the equation of exchange, and should expect to be able to keep the equation straight, in a great variety of situations, by allowing the V's to vary.

Before undertaking detailed analysis of the causes governing V, I shall discuss Fisher's specific argument, typical of the quantity theory, that an increase of money cannot change the V's. "As a matter of fact, the velocities of circulation of money and deposits depend, as we have seen, on technical conditions, and bear no discoverable relation to the quantity of money in circulation. Velocity of circulation is the average rate of 'turnover,' and depends on countless individual rates of turnover. These, as we have seen, depend on individual *habits*. Each person regulates his turnover to suit his individual *convenience*.... In the long run, and for a large number of people, the average rate of turnover, or what amounts to the same thing, the average time money remains in the same hands, will be closely determined. It will depend on density of population, commercial *customs*, rapidity of transport, and other technical conditions, but not on the quantity of money and deposits nor on the price-level." (Italics mine.[208]) He proceeds to assume that money is doubled with a *halving* of the V's, instead of a *doubling* of P. Everybody now has on hand twice as much money *and deposits* as his convenience has taught him to keep on hand. He will then try to get rid of this surplus, and he can only do it by buying goods. But this will increase somebody else's surplus, and he will likewise try to get rid of it. This will raise prices. "*Obviously* this tendency will continue until there if found another adjustment of quantities to expenditures, and the *V's are the same as originally*."[209] The foregoing argument rests in part, it will be seen, on the assumption that a fixed ratio between M and M′ obtains, else the increase of *money* in everybody's hands would not mean a corresponding increase in their *deposits*. I have already criticised this doctrine. For the contention that the V's will finally be *just the same* as before, I find no specific argument at all—"*obviously*" presumably making that unnecessary.

As the point immediately at issue is that V's will be *unchanged* by the increase in M (otherwise P would not increase *proportionately*—let us see if considerations can be adduced which will make this a little less "obvious." First, it will be noticed that Fisher, in the foregoing, in one sentence speaks of the matter as resting on *habit,* and in the next sentence, on *convenience*. He speaks, also, of business *custom*. Now it is important to note that habit and custom, on the one hand, and considerations of convenience on the other, do not necessarily coincide. Many habits and customs are highly inconvenient. And it is not at all likely that habit and custom should govern so highly complex a thing as the ratio between cash on hand and the price-level. Rather, in so far as custom and habit rule, one would expect them to relate to a simpler matter, namely, the *amount of cash on hand*. If the amount of cash kept on hand should remain controlled by habit, while the amount of money is increased, then V, instead of remaining unchanged, would actually be increased, unless the habits should be broken in on. I shall show in a moment that considerations of convenience would probably lead to a reduced V, in so far as individual turnover is concerned. But which tendency will prevail? Well, that will depend on the degree to which custom and habit rule as compared with considerations of convenience—*i. e.*, there would be no rule valid for all communities. That convenience would lead to a larger amount of money on hand—and I am following Fisher's temporary hypothesis that there has been no rise in prices prior to the movement to restore the V's to their old magnitudes—will appear from considerations like these. Few men have as much on hand as they would like to have, including both their cash in hand and their deposit balances. Most people have the tendency to hoard, though it is usually held in check by necessity. If money on hand be increased suddenly, without prices being increased, and without any prospect of increased incomes in the future—and there is nothing in Fisher's provisional hypothesis to call for increased incomes, as they could, in fact, come only from an increase in prices—why might not there be a considerable saving of money, with a corresponding reduction in V? If it be objected that people, in saving their money, will in considerable degree put it into the banks, and that the banks, with larger reserves, will increase loans and deposits, I would urge, that it is on the part of banks that this tendency to increase hoards in times of abundant money is particularly marked, and for proof would point to the figures quoted from Keynes[210] for the great banks and treasuries of Europe in the last fifteen years. It is not necessary for my purpose at this point to do more than show that there is reason to expect an increase in money to *change* the V's. Fisher's argument rests on the contention that the V's will be neither increased or reduced—otherwise an increase in money will not *proportionately* raise prices. The appeal to habit and custom in the matter is particularly unsatisfactory. Custom and habit could not possibly regulate things so complex as velocities of money and bank-deposits.

Whatever be the ultimate effect of an increase in money, the immediate effect is commonly to reduce the money-rates. Banks have less inducement to pay interest on deposits, and charge lower rates for loans. Now merchants, especially small merchants, are often embarrassed in making change for customers. The man who has tried to make payment with a ten dollar bill in a country store has not infrequently put the storekeeper to much inconvenience. To offer a ten dollar bill, or even a five dollar bill, to a storekeeper on Amsterdam Avenue in New York City may well mean that the one clerk in the establishment, or the proprietor's wife will run out with the bill to three or four neighboring stores before finding change with which to break it. If money is more abundant, if money-rates are easier, for a time, it may easily happen that many small merchants will experience the superior convenience of having a more adequate amount of change in the till, and will, even after the money-rates have risen—if they do rise again to the old figure—find a new reason for keeping more cash on hand. There is a marginal equilibrium between the interest on the capital invested in cash in the till, and the wages of the clerk,[211] whose active legs assist the velocity of money. Not only banks and small dealers, however, find it advantageous to increase their supply of ready funds, held idle for special occasions. The United States Steel Corporation has kept as much as $50,000,000.00 to $75,000,000.00 in idle cash or idle deposits, as a means of being independent of banks in times of emergency.[212] The motive for accumulating reserves and hoards, either of cash or deposit accounts, is at all times strong. In times of financial ease, it may easily find the difficulties which ordinarily repress it give way, and, by being gratified, grow stronger.

I conclude that there is positive reason for expecting an increase of money to reduce the velocity of money.

Horace White, in his *Money and Banking,* in the earlier editions, speaks of the velocity of money, "*alias* the state of trade." Is not this the truth? Is not money circulating rapidly, when business is active, and slowly when business is dull? Is not the velocity of circulation a highly flexible and variable average, a *cause* of nothing, and an index of business activity? Or, better, perhaps, are not the V's and T both governed, in large degree, by more fundamental causes which are largely the same for both? Fisher would admit something of this for transition periods. Even for normal adjustments, he admits that an increase in T, unaccompanied by an increase in M, leads to some increase in the V's, though he doesn't say how much.[213] He denies, however, that an increase in the V's will increase T.[214] In general, it is clear that he regards the V's and T as governed by different causes. The control of the V's by T is not the only or the chief control of the V's. The V's can increase greatly without an increase of T, in his scheme. That this is so, will appear from a comparison of the list of causes which he gives as governing the V's and T respectively:

Causes governing V's:

1. Habits of the individual.
    (a) As to thrift and hoarding.
    (b) As to book credit.
    (c) As to use of checks.

2. Systems of payments in the community.
    (a) As to frequency of receipts and disbursements.
    (b) As to regularity of receipts and disbursements.
    (c) As to correspondence between times and amounts of receipts and disbursements.

3. General causes.
    (a) Density of population.
    (b) Rapidity of transportation.

Compare this list with the causes governing T:[215]

1. Conditions affecting producers: Geographical differences in Natural Resources; the division of labor; knowledge of technique of production; accumulation of capital.

2. Conditions affecting consumers: the extent and variety of human wants.

3. Conditions connecting consumers and producers:
    (a) Facilities for transportation.
    (b) Relative freedom of trade.
    (c) *Character* of monetary and banking systems. (Not their *extent*.)
    (d) Business confidence.

These two lists are quite different, and indicate that in Fisher's mind the magnitudes, T and the V's, in general obey different laws. The only factor in both lists is facilities for transportation ("rapidity of transportation," in the first list). Strangely enough, T, though later recognized as having influence on the V's[216] is not included in these lists in ch. 5. The "character of the monetary and banking systems" in the second list is evidently not the same as "use of checks" in the second list, though it will doubtless affect that factor, as also the "habits as to thrift and hoarding," in some degree. "Business confidence," which is, in the view I am maintaining, as in the view, I should take it, of Horace White, the great variable affecting both T and the V's, does not appear in the first list. Indeed, one wonders why business confidence appears in either list, if only "normal," and not merely "transitional" causes are to be considered, but it appears from the fuller discussion on p. 78 that Fisher is not thinking of business confidence as a *variable* at all—his normal theory has nothing to do with *variables*—but as a thing which either is or is not present, a sort of Mendelian unit, not a thing of degrees.[217] It will be noted, further, that most of the causes which Fisher lists as affecting T are really causes affecting *production*—they would be just as important under a socialistic as under an exchange economy.

Now I propose to show, on the basis of Fisher's own list of causes, that most, if not all, of the factors affecting the V's, will also affect T, *and in the same direction*. He admits this as to transportation facilities. It is surely true of thrift and hoarding. The miser neither circulates money nor buys goods. It is emphatically true—though Fisher's theory, as will later appear, is obliged to deny it,—of both book credit and banking facilities. Without the use of credit, much of the business now done simply would not be done at all. For Fisher, and the quantity theory in general, the contention would be simply that the same business would be done *on a lower price-level.* I reserve a full discussion of this fundamental point till later, noting here, in passing, that the function of banks is to assist in effecting transfers, that that is why, from the social standpoint, banks are encouraged, and that the extension of banking would be folly if they did not, in fact, do this. As to book credit, let us suppose that, for example, in the great cotton section of the South the stores should cease to give advances of supplies on credit to negroes and small white farmers, pending the "making" of the crop. The outcome would be starvation for many of them, and no cotton crop at all. Under a system of private enterprise, the very division of labor itself, including the specialization of the capitalist, involves credit, and it is difficult to conceive a form of credit which does not either dispense with the use of money, or increase its "velocity." Admittedly, the division of labor increases trade.

The three factors listed under "Systems of payment in the community" also affect trade. To the extent that receipts are frequent, regular, and synchronous with outgo, we have a smoothly working economic system, which facilitates commerce.

Finally, density of population enormously increases trade. The concentration of men in cities is essential for modern factory production, and the great cities have necessarily grown up about good harbors, or at strategic points for connecting lines of railroads. It seems almost trivial to insist on so obvious a point, but Fisher seems totally to ignore it, for he says: "We conclude, then, that density of population and rapidity of transportation have tended to increase prices by raising velocities. *Historically this concentration of population in cities has been an important factor in raising prices in the United States.*"[218] (P. 88. Italics mine.)

This is an astounding proposition. It is not merely that the concentration of population in cities has *tended* to raise prices through raising velocities. It is a statement that this has been an important historical cause of the actual increase in prices. For Fisher's own theory, if the same cause had tended to increase T,[219] that would have offset the rising V's on the other side of the equation, and left prices little affected. But he sees in the V's an independent cause here, divorces them from their connection with T, and follows his logic fearlessly where it leads. I do not see how one could more strikingly illustrate the essential vice of erecting the V's into causal entities.

In concluding the discussion of the rôle of velocity of circulation, I think it worth while to mention Fisher's own efforts to measure them. I examine his statistics in a later chapter. I do not regard the points at issue as points which can properly be handled by inductive methods, primarily. I do not accept his conclusions with reference to the magnitudes of V, the velocity of money, partly because I do not accept his doctrine that "banks are the home of money" (p. 287).[220] He finds for V a fairly constant magnitude during the thirteen years from 1896 to 1909, the range being from 19 to 22, the figures for all the years except 1896 and 1909 being interpolations.[221] For V, however, which is much the more important magnitude, from the standpoint of his equation of exchange for the United States, since deposits do so much more exchanging than does money, he finds a wide range of variation, from 36 to 54, and he states: "We note that the velocity of circulation has increased 50% in thirteen years and that it has been subject to great variation from year to year. In 1899 and 1906 it reached maxima, immediately preceding crises" (285). I think Fisher's own statistical results show that V´, at least, is a child of the "state of trade."[222] Critical analysis of these statistics show that they greatly underestimate the variability of the V's.[223]

In summary: V and V´ are not, as Fisher contends, independent of the quantity of money. Instead of resting on "technical conditions," and having large elements of constancy and rigidity, they are highly flexible, and vary, on the whole, with the same highly complex and divergent sets of causes which govern the volume of trade. The biggest factor affecting the variations of the V's on the one hand, and volume of trade on the other is business confidence—a factor which Fisher's normal theory is not concerned with, so far as it is considered as a variable, but which, more than anything else, does affect the concrete figures which go into the equation of exchange, either for a single year, or for an average of a good many years. The V's are not true causal entities, but merely abstract summaries of a host of heterogeneous facts. I have indicated before, and shall later demonstrate more fully, that the same is true of T. Even the "normal" causes governing the V's, however, are factors which likewise affect T, and in the same direction.

Among the factors affecting both V and T, there is one which sometimes makes them move in opposite directions, and that is the *value of money* itself. This is so well stated in Wicksteed's interesting criticism of the quantity theory that I content myself with a quotation:[224] "Again, the history of paper money abounds in instances of sudden changes, within the country itself, in the value of paper currency, caused by reports unfavorable to the country's credit. The value of the currency was lowered in these cases by a doubt as to whether the Government would be permanently stable and would be in a position to honor its drafts, that is to say, whether this day three months, the persons who have the power to take my goods for public purposes will accept a draft of the present Government in lieu of payment. It is not easy to see how, on the theory of the quantity law, such a report could affect very rapidly the magnitudes on which the value of the note is supposed to depend, viz., the quantity of business to be transacted, and the amount of the currency. Nor is it easy to see why we should suppose that the frequency with which the notes pass from hand to hand, is independently fixed. On the other hand, the quantity of business done by the notes, as distinct from the quantity of business done altogether, and the rapidity of the circulation of the notes may obviously be affected by sinister rumors. Two of the quantities, then, supposed to determine the value of the unit of circulation, are themselves liable to be determined by it."